MW00425601

To:
From:
Date:

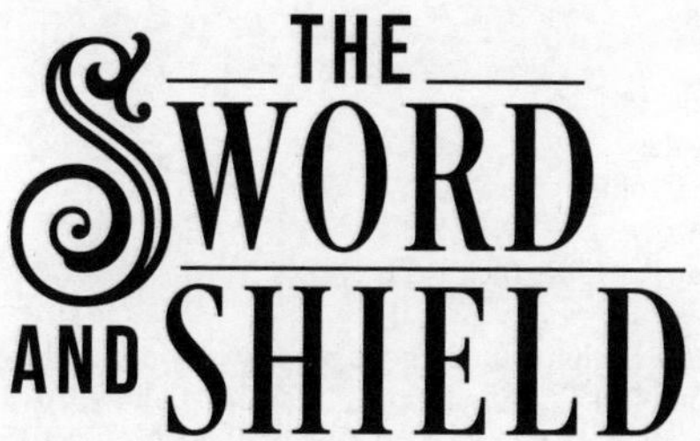
THE
SWORD
AND SHIELD

Visit Christian Art Gifts, Inc. at www.christianartgifts.com.

The Sword and Shield: A 40-day Devotional Journey for Men

Written by Robert Noland
Edited by Christy Distler
Design by Annabelle Grobler

Published by Christian Art Gifts Inc., IL, USA

ISBN: 978-1-63952-406-8

Printed in China

28 27 26 25 24 23
10 9 8 7 6 5 4 3 2 1

The Sword and Shield

A 40-DAY DEVOTIONAL JOURNEY FOR MEN

Robert Noland

Contents

Before You Begin

From biblical to medieval times, the sword was primarily an offensive weapon with the shield used for defense. In the dominant hand of the warrior, the sword was wielded to advance while in the lesser hand, the shield defended against attacks. Both were equal and necessary to survive in battle and achieve victory.

As modern metaphors for the Christian man in today's world, the sword represents spiritual growth — transformation into the image of Christ — and the shield, moral protection — proactive efforts to stop the Enemy's attacks. As examples, the commitment to daily prayer is a sword, while accountability with other men to strengthen areas of weakness is a shield.

One of my favorite Bible verses is Mark 1:35.

Very early in the morning, while it was still dark, Jesus got up, left the house and went off to a solitary place, where he prayed. (NIV)

To understand the meaning of this verse, you don't have to study the Greek language because it means exactly what it says in any translation or paraphrase you read. Jesus got up early in the morning and went away alone to pray for a single, simple purpose — to spend one-on-one time with His Father. We clearly see here from His example that a dedicated daily time alone with God is one of the most life-changing spiritual disciplines we can invest in. No distractions, devices, or noise, and no one else around — just you and God.

We are so glad you have chosen to spend the next forty days in *The Sword & Shield Men's Devotional*. Here are a few points we hope will encourage you as you begin your experience:

1. **Decide to commit**

   Plan to use this book for the next forty days, setting aside intentional and undistracted time to create a habit of engaging with God daily. If you miss a day or two, just pick back up where you left off. Please don't give in to the temptation to feel any guilt; just get back on board. This is not intended to be a religious exercise but an effort to build a relationship. So don't quit — commit. Your friendship with Christ is worth every moment you invest.

2. **Pick a time**

   While spending a few moments alone with God first thing in the morning can be best to set the pace for your day, choose when will be optimum for your schedule. You may need to experiment a bit, but pick a time and stick with it. We will all make time for the things that matter most to us.

3. Choose a place

Just like Jesus in Mark 1:35, you need a quiet and peaceful setting. Pick the most comfortable place you can find, away from distractions. No phones. No devices. No TV and no one else around. Your environment is crucial for you to be focused as you engage with God.

4. Read

Take in all the content. Don't scan, as you would a text or email, but carefully read it like a personal letter, particularly the Bible verses. If you prefer to use your own version of Scripture each day, feel free to do so. Just look up the day's passage and read your Bible instead.

5. *Sword & Shield* Connecting Points

With each of the forty days there is a *Sword* and a *Shield* open-ended sentence for you to complete. The purpose is to help you connect the day's content to your own life. The more open and honest you are with yourself in your answers, the more opportunity you create for spiritual growth and moral protection. Choosing to take the time to dive in and commit several minutes to this section each day will help you discover and apply the Scriptural and spiritual truths to your own life. If you prefer, you can use your own journal rather than the space provided in the book. Allowing a few minutes to write down your feelings, thoughts, and prayers is a great way to add to this experience, processing what God is saying to you. When you complete these forty days and go back through what you have written, you will likely be able to *see* your growth.

6. Pray

Allow time to speak with God. Tell Him everything like you would a best friend. Just talk to Him. Say what's on your heart. Be honest. Be specific. No fancy spiritual language. If you have never really prayed before or are uncomfortable, very simple prayers are provided at the end of each day. Learning to pray or deepening in your prayers will revolutionize your life and spiritual growth. Keep praying throughout your day in an ongoing dialogue with your Heavenly Father. Remember, He goes everywhere with you.

7. Listen and Obey

Close your time in a few quiet moments to hear God speak (Psalm 46:10). Quiet your mind and heart. Pray Samuel's prayer: "Speak, Lord, for your servant is listening" (1 Samuel 3:9). You may feel a little strange at first as you sit and listen, but if you stick with this discipline, you will be amazed at what the Holy Spirit will say to you. Then obey and live out what He tells you. A suggested verse is offered at the close of each day should you decide to start memorizing Scripture (Psalm 119:11).

8. Using in a small group

Whether you each agree to work through a day prior to getting together to be ready to discuss or read the day's content out loud in the meeting, spend the bulk of your time talking through the *Sword & Shield* page as your discussion questions. Accountability questions are also provided at the end of the book. Close by praying for one another.

Hold up the SHIELD OF FAITH to stop the fiery arrows of the devil. Put on SALVATION as your HELMET, and take the Sword of the SPIRIT, which is the WORD of God.

Ephesians 6:16-17

In the book's introduction, we talked about the distinctly different purposes between a sword and a shield in regard to offense and defense. On this first day, we'll look at a more modern version of how we can think about offense and defense to dive deeper spiritually.

Professional team sports are a mainstay in our culture's entertainment. There's a strong likelihood that you follow at least one sport, even in the offseason. Whether eleven on the football field, nine on the baseball diamond, five on the court, or even the one NASCAR driver with the pit crew looking on, offense and defense are equally crucial aspects in any sport. A team can have an amazing offense, but if there is a weak defense, they can still lose. And vice versa. We all know that consistent winners *score* points on offense and *stop* points on defense.

God through His Word has given us thousands of life principles to live by — for offense and defense. Here are some examples:

In personal purity:

Offense — Psalm 51:10: *Create in me a pure heart, O God. Renew a loyal spirit within me.*

Defense — Psalm 119:37, 39: *Turn my eyes from worthless things … Help me abandon my shameful ways.*

"Create" and "renew" are proactive words of offense, while "turn my eyes" and "help me abandon" are phrases of defense. These prayers ask God, paraphrasing, "help me begin these activities, while helping me stop these others." Change always requires starting new things while simultaneously stopping or ending old things. God will provide His "new" to replace the "old" we give up. Offense leads us into good and defense helps us stay away from evil.

In your relationships:

Offense — Proverbs 27:17: *As iron sharpens iron, so a friend sharpens a friend.*

Defense — Proverbs 3:27: *Do not withhold good from those who deserve it when it's in your power to help them.*

Spiritual sharpening is offense, while being careful to not withhold good is defense.

In your worship:

Offense — Psalm 95:6: *Come, let us bow down in worship, let us kneel before the LORD our Maker.*

Defense — Matthew 5:23-24: "*So if you are presenting a sacrifice at the altar in the Temple and you suddenly remember that someone has something against you, leave your sacrifice there at the altar. Go and be reconciled to that person. Then come and offer your sacrifice to God."*

Maintaining reconciliation is the defense clearing the field for your offense to bow and kneel, moving your faith forward.

In spiritual growth:

Offense — Psalm 46:10: *Be still, and know that I am God!*
Defense — Ephesians 4:31: *Get rid of all bitterness, rage, anger, harsh words, and slander, as well as all types of evil behavior.*

As your defense "gets rid of," your offense can "be still and know."

This offense/defense strategy is essentially a Bible study method that can help you place spiritual principles into your life. For any area where you have temptations or struggles and want to engage new patterns of behavior, find offensive and defensive Scriptures to support you. Once you find your own, place them in familiar places you see every day. Memorize them for application.

One of the greatest spiritual weapons we can wield is the incredible power of Scripture — both offensively to grow in the faith and defensively to defeat temptation and sin. Isaiah 55:11 states: *"It is the same with my word. I send it out, and it always produces fruit. It will accomplish all I want it to, and it will prosper everywhere I send it."*

Find and write down a favorite verse that best describes your spiritual offense for where you are in your life right now. Try to memorize the verse or passage.

Find and write down a favorite verse that best describes your spiritual defense for where you are in your life right now. Try to memorize the verse or passage.

"Heavenly Father, thank You for Your Word and how it works so powerfully in my life. Teach me to know You through Your Word and let Your truths go into my heart and flow out of my words and actions to others — changing me and changing the world."

Memory Verse

It is the same with my word. I send it out, and it always produces fruit. It will accomplish all I want it to, and it will prosper everywhere I send it.

- Isaiah 55:11-

OFFENSE IS spiritual growth.

DEFENSE IS moral protection.

PARTICIPATE DAY 2 PASSIVE

The TV and the internet are two primary sources of our society's information and entertainment. Watching TV, we sit back at a reasonable distance and just scan the channels to find what we want to view. We are consumers of TV's content, while we actually interact with the internet. To use a sports analogy, with TV you are in the stands, but you're on the field with the internet.

Other unique differences are TV stations are on 24/7, moving on in their standard programming with or without you. Unless you record a show, you will miss it and then must find another method or time to view the content. But with the internet, the site is always available for you to engage at your discretion. TV has its own schedule, and websites are on your schedule.

With TV, you have nothing to do with the outcome. With the internet, you decide every detail that takes place — when, where, what, and how long, with you controlling the experience. Of course, today with smart TVs, subscription services, and on-demand apps, TV programming is moving further away from the traditional model and more into the internet ecosystem. But one fact we have all come to accept: we are far more influenced now by the culture of the internet than that of TV.

After thinking through these basic differences in these two media, we can apply this same terminology to ourselves as Christ followers and ask, "In my relationship with God, am I a passive at-a-distance consumer or a close-up participant?" Consider these questions:

- Do I consistently get alone to commit some time to sit in the presence of God, seeking to engage in my relationship with Him?
- Do I most often pray with an agenda of only offering my list of needs and wants, or do I actually share my heart with Him?
- As I read God's Word, do I anticipate that His Spirit will intersect and interact with my spirit?
- With the people God places in my life, do I stand back at a distance, guarding myself, or do I proactively engage, caring about what is going on in their lives?

These candid questions are simply intended as an honest evaluation of whether you are taking full advantage of the deeply personal relationship that God offers through Jesus Christ. Answering tough questions with authentic transparency can lead us to real change.

We have the clear choice every day to approach life like a TV show — "Doesn't matter what I do. It's just going to move on with or without me." Or like the internet — "I'm going to engage with God and those around me in a unique experience every time."

Throughout the book of Hebrews, the message we find that Christ is the great High Priest who offered the final sacrifice for us all is a spiritual game changer. The writer invites us to engage in a deep relationship with God where every barrier has been destroyed and the path has been cleared from the moment of salvation into eternity.

So then, since we have a great High Priest who has entered heaven, Jesus the Son of God, let us hold firmly to what we believe. This High Priest of ours understands our weaknesses, for he faced all of the same testings we do, yet he did not sin. So let us come boldly to the throne of our gracious God. There we will receive his mercy, and we will find grace to help us when we need it most. (Hebrews 4:14–16)

In my relationship with God, one way that I can be more proactive and intentional is to:

In my relationship with God, one roadblock or hindrance that I must determine to get rid of is:

"Lord Jesus, empower me to be a close-up participant in the life You designed and ordained me to live when You created me and mapped out all my days. Thank You for inviting me to join You in changing the world — today. I want to come humbly yet boldly before Your throne to find the mercy and grace I need to both receive and give today."

Memory Verse

So let us come boldly to the throne of our gracious God. There we will receive his mercy, and we will find grace to help us when we need it most.

- Hebrews 4:16 -

Wherever you are,
be all THERE.

Most of us have memories of learning to ride a bike as a kid. Life was so free and easy when the training wheels were bolted on the sides. But when the decision was made to take them off and try to learn to balance, everything changed. Our minds told us there was no possible way we could ever stay upright on those two wheels. The fear and anticipation of a bad spill was always there.

But at the same time, we could see ourselves sailing down the sidewalk, the wind blowing on our faces in a newfound freedom on the bike. So after crashing and crying with a few skinned knees and elbows, faith finally won out over fear. The dream was realized and for the rest of our lives, we know how to ride a bike. We found the balance and faith brought flight.

The great thing about learning to ride a bike during our formative years is that this same scenario plays out over and over in different ways throughout our lives, and most often with much higher stakes. An opportunity emerges and we have to learn how to balance life in a new way. We somehow find the faith to overcome overwhelming fear. When people are depending on us, our decision of whether to push through or give up is critical. Maybe God has called us to something we've never done before or never thought we would face. We arrive at a crossroads and the direction we take determines the future — literally.

Fear can quickly overtake the mind when faith has not yet overcome the heart. And one or the other — faith or fear — will end up being the clear winner. The two don't — and won't — co-exist. The proverbial deathbed is the final evaluation of the moments in life when faith or fear won out. The victories recalled are from faith and the regrets felt come from when fear ruled the day.

There are amazing moments in our lives when faith rises up, making us feel unstoppable. God is in the house and we know it! But then there are those times when we feel the questions come; the doubts overwhelm, and the what-if's scream at us. Fear creeps in to say we're going to make a mistake … again. And then the real question comes: "God, where did *You* go? Did You leave and that's why I feel like all the hope just got sucked out of my heart?"

We must always remember that God doesn't move away from us; we move away from Him. We *choose* fear over faith. We allow doubt to overcome our minds when we have just as much opportunity to let faith overpower our hearts.

There is only One who can bring real faith and hope to us and at the same time run fear out of town. His name is Jesus. Whether you're experiencing debilitating fear or overcoming faith today, running to Him is the best decision you can make.

I prayed to the Lord, and he answered me. He freed me from all my fears. Those who look to him for help will be radiant with joy; no shadow of shame will darken their faces. In my desperation I prayed, and the Lord listened; he saved me from all my troubles. For the angel of the Lord is a guard; he surrounds and defends all who fear him. Taste and see that the Lord is good. Oh, the joys of those who take refuge in him! Fear the Lord, you his godly people, for those who fear him will have all they need. Even strong young lions sometimes go hungry, but those who trust in the Lord will lack no good thing. (Psalm 34:4–10)

I can best express my faith in Christ today by:

The fear I most want to overcome today is:

"Father, I want to leave fear behind and walk in faith today so I choose You. May my life honor You as my heart is filled with Your hope."

MEMORY VERSE

EVEN STRONG YOUNG LIONS SOMETIMES GO HUNGRY, BUT THOSE WHO TRUST IN THE LORD WILL LACK NO GOOD THING.

- PSALM 34:10 -

Fear IS AN illusion WE CAN BECOME wrongly convinced IS A REALITY.

Faith IS A reality WE CAN BECOME wrongly convinced IS AN ILLUSION.

"Yeah, I'm hoping to have that project on your desk by the end of the week."
"I know I can have the work finished by sometime next month."
"My plan is to start just as soon as possible."
"When I can get everything to fall into place, I'll be ready to go."
"Once I can get past the next three months, I should be able to be home more."

Do these phrases sound familiar at all? When we make vague statements without specifics, we intend to sound highly proactive and as hopeful as possible. We can try to come off like we're making promises without actually creating a commitment. But how often is this just disguised procrastination or desperate diversions? They may be *well-meaning* but all too often they become *misleading* to everyone. And the tragedy comes when we start to also mislead ourselves.

Honestly, the difference can come down to our motives. Our ultra-busy, rapid-fire, get-it-done-at-all-cost culture has transformed the tyranny of the urgent into the new status quo. Today, mere activity is often allowed to be a replacement for excellence.

In contrast, when we look at Scripture, we see that God never *intends* to do anything. He either *does* something or *doesn't*. He always follows through with His words and actions. What He promises in the future takes place with a 100 percent accuracy rate — the result of perfection we cannot comprehend.

But fortunately for us, this also means that God won't forgive halfway, love just a little, get something almost finished, or forget to bless us. With God, He's all or none, but always intentional. Everything is on purpose. With His Spirit in us as His followers, we have access to these same amazing attributes. While we will never achieve perfection, the great news is we have the choice to yield to His nature over our own.

In light of these thoughts:

- Would you describe your average day as accidental or intentional?
- Do most events in your life happen *to* you or because *of* you?
- How could your days be lived with more intentionality?
- What if you could stop allowing current circumstances or momentary feelings to influence and sometimes manipulate your actions?
- How might your life improve if consistently "yes meant yes" and "no meant no"?
- What if only your calling from God determined your calendar?

Let's ask the question from a different angle: How much do you *plan* versus how much do you *perform*? Try this experiment for the next several days: Evaluate what you plan against what you actually perform or accomplish. If things regularly change between your plan and performance then what intervened? Was it because you made a choice to avoid something, or simply pursued a different path?

Living a life of integrity means:

- Growing in consistency and clarity in your actions
- Operating by God's plan rather than focusing on mere performance in the moment
- Lining up intention with action
- Becoming consistent in your character everywhere

The more the hand of God guides our steps, the steadier and straighter we will walk. The Scripture passage today is written with both intention and intensity about God's heart for us.

We can make our own plans, but the Lord gives the right answer. People may be pure in their own eyes, but the Lord examines their motives. Commit your actions to the Lord, and your plans will succeed. ... We can make our plans, but the Lord determines our steps. (Proverbs 16:1–3, 9)

Today, my priority to be proactive must involve (people or places):

Today, I will avoid procrastination with/in (people/places/circumstances):

"Jesus, Your life was always intentional with purpose. Help me to line up my intentions with action to be pleasing in Your sight. Help me to plan and then perform only as You would have me. May Your purpose become my reputation."

Memory Verse

We can make our plans, but
the Lord determines our steps.

- Proverbs 16:9 -

Pray.
PLAN.
Purpose.
PERFORM.

Someone once coined the phrase “God’s waiting room,” meaning a season in our lives when He is doing work *on* us to produce an eternal work *in* us, so He can later do a greater work *through* us. He temporarily places us in a holding pattern to accomplish His purposes.

This concept is seen in John 15 where Jesus said we are branches on His vine, and God will stop and prune us so we can eventually bear His fruit. Pruning takes time, care, and waiting for the careful cutting to be done.

For busy, impatient humans, soon all waiting becomes difficult because the very nature of the condition means you don’t know when your circumstance will change. And then the questions always eventually come: “What is God waiting on? Why am I waiting at all? What does He want from me? What did I do wrong?” Most often at some point, the Accuser shows up and whispers to us, “If you were really valuable to Him and His kingdom, you wouldn’t be here, now would you? No one else you know is waiting like this. You must have really messed up this time.”

In the Bible, the best example of this difficult season is in the story of Job. He was actually on death's door in the ER waiting room, listening to criticism, waiting on God. And then the Almighty showed up and a very candid conversation took place. Here is the outcome of Job's waiting experience.

Then Job replied to the Lord: "I know that you can do anything, and no one can stop you. You asked, 'Who is this that questions my wisdom with such ignorance?' It is I — and I was talking about things I knew nothing about, things far too wonderful for me. You said, 'Listen and I will speak! I have some questions for you, and you must answer them.' I had only heard about you before, but now I have seen you with my own eyes." (Job 42:1–5)

Job was essentially saying, in paraphrase, "I went on and on, demanding answers, which You did not give me. But in the end, instead of getting my questions answered, I got You, God. Now, instead of my friends' secondhand info, I have firsthand experience with You!" Job had an eternal opportunity arise out of a horrific temporary state.

But how often are we sitting in circumstances made by our own hands and God is just waiting on our questions to stop so He can give us an actual answer? We can be so quick to get angry and complain when life becomes uncomfortable and challenging. We quickly ask, "Why, God?" when we should actually be praying, "Work, God!" Not a spoiled-child demand, but a faith-saturated request from an adopted son.

There are certainly times when it is absolutely necessary and perfectly understandable to ask God, "Why?" However, asking Him time and time again, while not moving forward and seeking His heart can become a pity party, if we're not careful.

So is there a place in your life where it's high time to stop asking, "Why, God?" and start praying, "Work, God!"? Begin asking Him to work in, around, and all over your life; stop focusing on the apparent lack of activity in the physical world and start seeing His proactivity in the spiritual realm. We have the same opportunity as Job to say, *"I know that you can do anything, and no one can stop you,"* and finally confess, *"but now I have seen you with my own eyes."*

Father, I need to see You work today in:

Father, please forgive me for demanding to know "why?" in:

"Heavenly Father, waiting is always hard, so help me to submit to Your hand when You're working on me to accomplish Your purposes and work through me. I want You to use my life for Your plan in Your will."

Memory Verse

"I had only heard about you before, but now I have seen you with my own eyes."

- Job 42:5 -

ACCEPT THAT *God* ALONE
MAY KNOW THE WHYS,
BUT *He* WILL
ALWAYS
invite AND
involve
YOU IN *His* WORK.

INTENTION DAY 6 IMPULSE

You're driving to a meeting in the midst of a busy day. You glance over and see a Starbucks and, within seconds, you're the ninth car in the drive-thru. You're killing time online, just clicking around, and within ten minutes, you've made a purchase you had no plans to make. Running into the grocery store on the way home for a couple of necessities, you somehow end up in the checkout line with your plastic carry basket full. And then you find yourself surrounded by candy bars on all sides, justifying the hungry distance between the drive home and dinnertime.

Our fast-paced culture, coupled with the barrage of retail and online choices, has created constant distractions, ongoing temptations, and continuous complications that past generations never dreamed possible.

Take a moment to ask yourself:

- Is my day-to-day life driven primarily by impulse or intention?
- By whim or wisdom? By want or need?
- Do my thoughts tend to be impulsive or intentional?
- Are my decisions typically impulsive or intentional?

Impulse is reactive. Intention is proactive. Impulse is an immediate response. Intention is a calculated response. We tend to lean toward one or the other. Someone once said, "As go the hours of our days, so goes our life." So how do you change from an impulsively driven life to an intentional one? Here are a few simple helps:

1. **Slow down**

   A busy, fast-paced, and chaotic lifestyle creates impulsive decisions because there is typically little to no time left to be intentional. The only way a speeding car can stop is to slam on the brakes or crash. If you feel like you can't bring life to a halt or at least slow down, maybe it's time to ask yourself who actually has control of life's gas pedal?

2. **Think for yourself**

   Allowing external forces to make decisions for us today is actually quite simple to do. What someone just texted, emailed, posted, called about, or personally delivered as your next crisis makes you feel you must respond now. Or at the very least, an expectation comes where you feel you now have to shift your focus.

   Is anyone in your life thinking for you? Are you taking too many life cues from social media, a certain person, or other external source? Evaluate this seriously.

You might be surprised what you discover when you stop and get honest with yourself.

3. **Commit to Romans 12:1 — being a living sacrifice**

   Paul told all Christ followers that dying to self on a regular basis is to be an actual lifestyle, not merely a biblical suggestion. The "living sacrifice" is always alive yet always prepared to die, hence the name. The Holy Spirit can lead our lives when life is lived on the altar of God. We know this by looking at Jesus' choices in the Gospels. Yes, for us temptation will come and sin will happen. But forgiveness comes quickly when we crawl off our throne and make the choice to get back on His altar — where the impulse can die and the intentional life can be lived.

And so, dear brothers and sisters, I plead with you to give your bodies to God because of all he has done for you. Let them be a living and holy sacrifice — the kind he will find acceptable. This is truly the way to worship him. Don't copy the behavior and customs of this world, but let God transform you into a new person by changing the way you think. Then you will learn to know God's will for you, which is good and pleasing and perfect. (Romans 12:1–2)

Father, I make the choice today to be intentional in/with:

so please give me the boldness and strength today to:

God, I need help today to stop or slow down in/with:

so please help me fight the impulse to:

"Father God, please help me to slow down. Teach me to think as You would have me, and offer up my life to You for You to live through me. Help me to live intentionally."

MEMORY VERSE

DON'T COPY THE BEHAVIOR AND CUSTOMS OF THIS WORLD, BUT LET GOD TRANSFORM YOU INTO A NEW PERSON BY CHANGING THE WAY YOU THINK. THEN YOU WILL LEARN TO KNOW GOD'S WILL FOR YOU, WHICH IS GOOD AND PLEASING AND PERFECT.

- ROMANS 12:2 -

AS GO
THE *hours* OF OUR
DAYS, SO GOES
OUR *life.*

What if today you were offered the choice of great wealth or grounded wisdom? Which would you choose? Let's get specific as to how these two scenarios might look.

For wealth, let's say that at the beginning of each month, the exact amount that you spent the previous month was deposited into your account so that all your balances are paid to zero. Whatever life costs, you receive the money to pay the bills. Whatever you need will be supplied and there will always be enough. No need. No lack.

For wisdom, let's say that in any situation you encounter in life, no matter the issue or problem, you know exactly the right decision to make and the best option to take because you have all the wisdom you need. You always know the right course of action for *any* setting. No need. No lack.

There is no question that the vast majority of people today would choose wealth. We see this fact played out daily throughout our culture in so many ways. From the lottery jackpot to internet get-rich-quick schemes to crime, people want to gain wealth any way they can. The bottom line of so many motives always seems to be about money.

To add insult to injury, when people do come into actual wealth, so often they focus the full benefit of their new resources only on themselves. In fact, statistics tell us the average American gives only two to three percent of their annual income to charity and the higher the income, the lower the percentage given. The bottom line is the less you have, the more you tend to give away — the opposite of what we believe to be true. When we say, "If only I were wealthy, I'd help those people," the cold, hard fact is if we won't help at all now, we certainly won't if we have more money.

Therefore, wisdom would certainly benefit each of us in keeping life on the right track but would also be a blessing for everyone around us. The people we love and those we encounter daily would gain from our wise decisions. In fact, the argument could be made that someone with great wisdom could help others even more than themselves. After all, is wisdom truly wisdom unless it is shared? A wealthy person living in isolation can spend what they want on themselves and still stay rich, but a wise person living in seclusion with no outlet is allowing their greatest resource to be wasted.

Most of us will never experience the level of wealth to meet all of our many desires in life because even when more money comes, our list just increases. But the wisdom of God is available to us right now at any time for any need we have.

Wealth will burn, but wisdom will benefit and build up lives.

Make a practice of daily asking God to reveal His truth in any situation where you need a decision or direction, especially when it impacts others' lives.

But all too quickly the message is crowded out by the worries of this life, the lure of wealth, and the desire for other things, so no fruit is produced. (Mark 4:19)

If any of you lacks wisdom, you should ask God, who gives generously to all without finding fault, and it will be given to you. (James 1:5 NIV)

How much better to get wisdom than gold, and good judgment than silver! (Proverbs 16:16)

Lord, I need Your wisdom today in these specific situations:

Lord, I confess that wealth with its desires and temptations have affected me negatively in these areas:

"Father, it seems like so much of life is about working hard and seeking wealth. But as I work, when I am at home, anywhere I am, I ask You to help me to grow in Your wisdom, to know Your mind and heart for any situation I find myself."

Memory Verse

If any of you lacks wisdom, you should ask God, who gives generously to all without finding fault, and it will be given to you.

- James 1:5 NIV -

WEALTH WILL *burn,* BUT WISDOM WILL *benefit* AND *build up* LIVES.

Input Day 8 Output

We all understand the concept of what we put into something is what will come out. And the opposite: nothing in means that nothing comes out. In fact, in some situations such as relationships, this actually produces not just a zero-sum but also a negative effect.

If you buy a new computer with a fresh, clean hard drive, within a year it will contain any and everything you have created, added, and accessed; however, if it just sits on your desk and is never used, it will remain empty. Your car can only burn the gas you put in the tank. Your body can only burn the calories you intake.

This law is true in most all areas of our lives — from the food we eat to the lies we believe. Only what goes in is what comes out.

Here's an interesting, ironic, and yes, often frustrating side of this concept for so many of us. Being lazy about what is actually going into our lives is easy. Therefore, we can spend a great deal of time expecting amazing things to happen when we have put in little to no effort. From our relationship with God to marriage to parenting to friends to career, we want to put in ten and get one hundred out. That is inherent in us all, created from a mixture of pride and passivity.

The good or bad news, depending on your perspective, is that the answer to this problem in us all is simply focus, discipline, and hard work. But with that, how can we get better at both input and output?

1. **Eliminate distractions**

   Identify what keeps derailing your input in your time with God, quality time with your family and friends, and time spent on what you are most passionate about.

2. **Engage realistic expectations**

   Ask, "Where am I expecting too much and too little of myself?" A natural tendency is to expect a great deal of others and too little of ourselves. So often we don't even realize we are imbalanced in our expectations. On the other hand, we can also easily beat ourselves up for not delivering all that we think we should.

3. **Embrace discipline**

   Pushing through and pressing on is often the best and only answer to many of life's dilemmas. Running away or ignoring them just creates more problems. In fact, facing them most often diminishes the fears.

4. **Redirect energy**

    Our culture can demand we place time and energy on the wrong things. Sitting down to reflect and map out where your time is spent might shed light on why your input and output are not optimum. Giving God full access and authority to your calendar could be the best move you could make. Surrender, pray, and let Him run your schedule for a week and see what happens. After all, He's your Creator.

5. **Yes and no are still sufficient answers**

    Giving firm yes or no answers according to what is right and best for the situation is still perfectly fine to do. Allowing others' expectations and approval to determine your decisions is problematic. This must particularly be addressed if you tend to be a people pleaser.

Jesus said, "The first in importance is, 'Listen, Israel: The Lord your God is one; so love the Lord God with all your passion and prayer and intelligence and energy.' And here is the second: 'Love others as well as you love yourself.' There is no other commandment that ranks with these." (Mark 12:29–31 MSG)

Father, I need more of Your *input* into these places in my life:

Father, I need Your help with my *output* in these places in my life:

"Almighty God, I ask for Your Spirit's help to access more of Your Word and be a filter of what comes into my life. Help me to reflect more of You for others to see."

Memory Verse

And you must love the Lord your God with all your heart, all your soul, all your mind, and all your strength."

- Mark 12:30 -

Giving GOD FULL AUTHORITY AND access TO YOUR CALENDAR WOULD BE THE best move YOU COULD EVER make.

INFLUENCE DAY 9 ISOLATION

As followers of Jesus, the big picture for us is to join Him in reaching the circles of influence He has given us. If you are like most men, you can tend to downplay your abilities and impact on the people around you. But reaching people anywhere, on any level, is how we can change the world — one heart at a time, just as He did. Maybe your chance to bring change will be in your home, workplace, neighborhood, or community.

Often today, our self-survival tendencies in the chaotic busyness of life pull us away from people and into isolation. Such a response originates from Adam and Eve's reaction to their sin in the garden after they had broken fellowship with God. They ran away and hid. For so many reasons, we can find it very easy to hide when life gets challenging or we know we need to take some sort of tough action we would prefer to avoid.

We can isolate ourselves in two ways. First, by our actual routine as we get into a rut of getting up, going to work, eating, sleeping, and then repeating the status quo. We may arrive at the place where we rarely venture outside the hamster wheel that we methodically created. Even church can become just another weekly to-do item on the list. And we may also falsely begin to believe that time spent on social media is human interaction.

The second way we isolate ourselves is that even though we may be around a lot of people we stay on the surface, never delving very deep into spiritual and emotional issues with anyone. Sure, we're with other humans, but we only talk about the weather, current events, and surface topics. Even the most extraverted person can actually become very isolated from the world because they never allow anyone to get past the mask of their personality.

Considering these thoughts, we can conclude that there can be no real influence while living in isolation. Likes and follows on social media, saying hi in the hallways, or nodding to folks in the neighborhood is not actual influence.

If you are a Christ follower, God intends for you to be *His* influence anywhere and everywhere you are, whether you naturally encounter five or five hundred people a day. And that influence can come *by* Him, *from* Him, and *through* Him.

While this responsibility and role to represent Christ can sometimes be hard for us to believe and accept, we are the best ambassadors for Him available to the people, places, and positions in the circles God has placed us. That is exactly why He calls *us* to be His witnesses, right where we are. There may be people in your life who literally no one else will be able to reach out to but you.

Always remember — we are called to live *out* our mission, not live *in* a mission. We are ministers, not monks.

All these new things are from God who brought us back to himself through what Christ Jesus did. And God has given us the privilege of urging everyone to come into his favor and be reconciled to him. For God was in Christ, restoring the world to himself, no longer counting men's sins against them but blotting them out. This is the wonderful message he has given us to tell others. We are Christ's ambassadors. God is using us to speak to you: we beg you, as though Christ himself were here pleading with you, receive the love he offers you — be reconciled to God. (2 Corinthians 5:18–20 TLB)

Father, please increase my influence for You in/with:

Father, I know I have isolated myself in/with:

so please give me the strength and boldness to reach out once again and engage by:

"God, guide me to find balance in my life, to be convicted of where I tend to isolate, and to be intentional about utilizing the places where You have blessed me with influence."

Memory Verse

For God was in Christ, restoring the world to Himself, no longer counting men's sins against them but blotting them out. This is the wonderful message He has given us to tell others.

- 2 Corinthians 5:19 TLB -

WE ARE CALLED TO *live* OUT OUR MISSION, NOT LIVE IN A *mission.*

"I really like his confidence. He's a good man."
"Wow, what an arrogant guy! Such a jerk."

Do you think these two quotes are about different people or the same person? While the answer could be correct either way, we all know we can be both of these men depending on the circumstances of any given moment in any given day.

The events that take place in our lives where we experience pride and victory can feel like a walk on a tightrope when expressing our feelings to others comes into play. The dance between confidence and arrogance can sometimes be confusing.

Here are some key points to compare and better understand the differences.

- Confidence tends to be quiet, while arrogance is usually loud.

Getting noisy about something we have done — however that looks for our specific personality, whether extraverted or introverted — usually means we have left confidence behind and moved on into the territory of arrogance. Those who choose to be quiet about a situation are rarely accused of being braggarts. *Arrogant know-it-alls stir up discord, but wise men and women listen to each other's counsel. (Proverbs 13:10 MSG)*

- Confidence welcomes others to speak, while arrogance interrupts.

Confident people actively listen to what others are saying, knowing their opportunity and timing to speak will be right. Arrogance appears to be listening but is actually just looking for the next opportunity to butt in and prove a point. *Pride first, then the crash, but humility is precursor to honor. Answering before listening is both stupid and rude. (Proverbs 18:12–13 MSG)*

- Confidence waits for others to recognize the victory, while arrogance announces the win to anyone who will listen.

Our praises sung always sound best from someone else's mouth. Confident folks have more fun waiting for others to discover the outcome. The true joy is found in the victory itself, not constantly replaying the story for others. *Love is patient and kind. Love is not jealous or boastful or proud. (1 Corinthians 13:4)*

- Confidence is a strong offense, while arrogance is a poor defense.

Anytime we speak and act arrogantly, this will always be a defensive tactic covering up for insecurities. Confidence is proactive. Arrogance is counteractive. *But let us who live in the light be clear-headed, protected by the armor of faith and love, and wearing as our helmet the confidence of our salvation. (1 Thessalonians 5:8)*

- Confidence is found in Christ, while arrogance comes from self.

Gaining the understanding that our identity and hope are in Christ can build a solid foundation of security and stability. The daily battle to surrender our own egos and allow only what He can produce in us will rid us of our arrogance and usher in His confidence. *Because of Christ and our faith in him, we can now come boldly and confidently into God's presence. (Ephesians 3:12) Arrogance and pride — distinguishing marks in the wicked — are just plain sin. (Proverbs 21:4 MSG)*

Even with all the countless books, talks, and online posts available today about believing in ourselves, being successful, and gaining self-confidence, we all struggle with self-image, self-doubt, and personal belief on some level. While developing a healthy self-esteem is a positive quality, our God-concept is much more crucial to avoiding arrogance from insecurities and finding confidence through our identity in Christ. *My heart is confident in you, O God; my heart is confident. (Psalm 57:7)*

Father, I know I can find my confidence in my relationship with You because:

Father, I confess I have struggled with arrogance in these places in my life:

"Almighty God, take away any arrogance from me today. Help me to live humbly as You did. I confess and declare the words of Psalm 57:7: 'My heart is confident in you, O God; my heart is confident.'"

Memory Verse

My heart is confident in you,
O God; my heart is confident.

- Psalm 57:7 -

OUR PRAISES sung ALWAYS SOUND best FROM SOMEONE ELSE'S mouth.

In 2 Kings 6 and 7, there is an amazing account of God's intervention with Elisha for God's people. At war with Israel, the Arameans surrounded Samaria, laying siege and cutting off all supply lines. The entire opposing army had set up camp nearby. Soon, there was no food left in the city and the people were literally starving to death. Israel's leaders were growing more hopeless by the day.

In 7:1, Elisha responds and tells them, *"Listen to this message from the LORD! This is what the LORD says: By this time tomorrow in the markets of Samaria, six quarts of choice flour will cost only one piece of silver, and twelve quarts of barley grain will cost only one piece of silver."*

Of course, predicting such an outcome seemed ridiculous based on their current circumstances. The prophet declaring that God's intervention would arrive within twenty-four hours with their desperate demand being met with such abundant supply sounded more like madness than a miracle.

Meanwhile, four men with leprosy were sitting alone outside the city gate. As they began to weigh their options of going into the city or staying put, they knew both would end in certain death. So ironically, the only choice with a potential upside was to surrender by walking into the enemy camp. They decided the risk of being executed as enemies was worth the possibility of being fed as prisoners.

With night approaching, the four lepers got up and started walking toward their fate. As they got close to the enemy's camp, the Lord created the sound of a large army invading. The soldiers heard the thunderous noise, assumed an attack by a much larger force was at hand and ran for their lives, leaving everything behind.

By the time the four lepers arrived, they found the camp abandoned with all the food, drink, clothing, horses, gold, and silver they could ever want. After they ate their fill, changed into new clothes, and loaded up with their new treasure, their consciences reminded them of the starving people back in the city. They decided that keeping their discovery all to themselves was wrong, so they went back to tell the king. When the incredible news of deliverance and provision spread, the people rushed out to the camp and found all they needed there. God saved His people — yet again — just as Elisha had prophesied.

Second Kings 7:16 says, *"Then the people of Samaria rushed out and plundered the Aramean camp. So it was true that six quarts of choice flour were sold that day for one piece of silver, and twelve quarts of barley grain were sold for one piece of silver, just as the Lord had promised."*

Second Kings 7:18 repeats verse 1 and reminds us what Elisha had said just the day before when all hope was lost and the future looked bleak. Certain death was exchanged for abundant life. The enemy's threat was silenced by God's answer. With the Lord, what a difference a day makes!

There are so many times in life when circumstances close in and we feel threatened and fearful, seeing no way out. In those times, we can start to believe our only choice is to accept our fate and not risk faith for divine deliverance.

So when you feel hopeless, confused, weary, and afraid, let this Bible account remind you that God can change any futile circumstance quite quickly into a fertile environment. But sometimes, just like the lepers, a broken and desperate act of faith in simple surrender is required to give Him the opportunity to go to work and change everything. Like Moses told the people of God in Exodus 14:14, *"The* Lord *will fight for you; you need only to be still."(NIV)*

Father, I am desperate today for an answer regarding:

Father, I have been struggling to believe and trust you with/in:

"Almighty God, I confess I know what it feels like to lose hope in a seemingly desperate situation and think nothing can be done. Help me today to have the simple faith of those lepers, surrender to You, and believe You will always provide, even when I can't see Your hand in the moment."

Memory Verse

"The Lord will fight for you; you need only to be still."

- Exodus 14:14 NIV -

A **broken** AND DESPERATE **act** OF FAITH IN SIMPLE **surrender** CAN GIVE GOD THE **opportunity** TO GO TO WORK AND **change everything.**

We have all heard the age-old phrase "time is money," meaning anything regarding money is going to require our time — making, spending, or saving. For example, the vast majority of the workforce is paid a set wage per hour. Even salaried and self-employed workers factor the time spent at a job compared to the amount they are paid.

While the amount of money people make varies on a wide spectrum, time is the same for everyone. All of us operate inside the same twenty-four hours in every day. No matter where we live on the planet or the time zone where we reside, we all start each day with a brand-new supply of minutes without doing anything to earn them. No matter your income, status, nationality, or station in life, you get the same number of hours as everyone.

To the contrary, money is a resource we have to earn. Simply living life and meeting only our basic needs costs money. Our resources are constantly being spent and depleted, and most people never feel they have enough, regardless of the size of their paychecks. So the variables involving money are very, very different from the static and consistent nature of time.

With this concept in mind, let's connect time and money as an analogy to how we view God's grace. Let me explain.

God's grace may be like money to you — always feeling like you must earn your way to Him by "good" behavior. You struggle to view grace as a free gift offered in faith because you believe you don't deserve it. Grace to you feels constantly spent up, so you never think you have enough to overcome bad choices. And no matter how much forgiveness may be offered to you, you are always left feeling guilt because you focus on your sin, not Christ. Christians and non-Christians alike can view grace through this manmade filter.

But God's grace may be like time to you. Always available no matter how "good" or "bad" you are. Grace is freely given and received because of what Christ has done, not what you have or haven't done. Like the morning brings another twenty-four hours, there is also a fresh, new supply of grace provided every day. This is the biblical New Covenant model, provided because we can never be good enough but at the same time we can never do anything bad enough for God to abandon us.

If you view God's grace more like money, then the great news is that time is available to change your perspective.

God saved you by his grace when you believed. And you can't take credit for this; it is a gift from God. Salvation is not a reward for the good things we have done, so none of us can boast about it. (Ephesians 2:8–9)

Yet God, in his grace, freely makes us right in his sight. He did this through Christ Jesus when he freed us from the penalty for our sins. (Romans 3:24)

But there is a great difference between Adam's sin and God's gracious gift. For the sin of this one man, Adam, brought death to many. But even greater is God's wonderful grace and his gift of forgiveness to many through this other man, Jesus Christ. (Romans 5:15)

Father, I see Your grace in my life through:

Father, I struggle most with receiving and accepting Your grace when:

"Heavenly Father, thank You for the cross of Christ where grace was born out of His sacrifice for me. Forgive me when I make Your love something I have to earn and not the gift that You constantly offer. Teach me to live in the grip of Your mercy every moment of every day."

Memory Verse

God saved you by His grace when you believed. And you can't take credit for this; it is a gift from God.

- Ephesians 2:8 -

GOD'S *grace* ARRIVES, LIKE A BRAND-NEW MORNING, *every* TWENTY-FOUR HOURS—ALWAYS AVAILABLE *freely given,* WITH A FRESH, NEW SUPPLY *every day.*

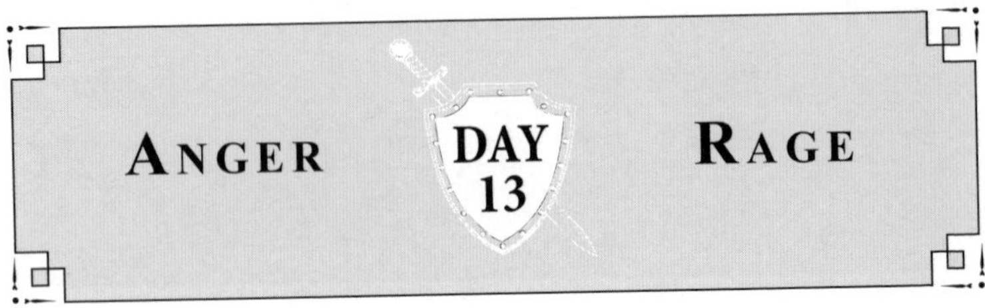

Anger — Day 13 — Rage

Our chaotic culture is most certainly turning out more angry people and, at the same time, offering more and more opportunity for people to suffer from rage. There's a reason we don't use the term "road anger," but rather "road *rage*." To start, let's understand the difference between anger and rage.

While we can all get frustrated from time to time while driving, incidents of road rage always have two major factors: First, the person is struggling with unresolved, pent-up anger, and second, a random traffic event simply acts as the trigger to release the boiling antagonism and irritation. The rage was already present when the person got in the car. The opportunity just presented itself while driving. In fact, the overwhelming anger may have actually begun with a family member at home or a boss at the office, but a total stranger will now bear the brunt of the wrath, regardless of whose fault became the actual catalyst.

Let's define rage as sudden verbal and physical outbursts fueled by anger. The picture is that of a lit fuse leading to an explosion. The angry moment simply lights it, leading to a blast of emotion. Anger…ssssssssssssssssss…RAGE! The deeper the anger and shorter the fuse, the bigger the rage. There can be plenty of times the fuse is lit, but something intervenes in time to snuff it out. Yet in other situations, the fire reaches the source and the damage is done.

Unresolved anger stuffed and pushed down into the heart will eventually produce rage. For that person, the flame is always waiting to touch the fuse. This is exactly why emotional explosions happen so quickly out of nowhere. And precisely why violence is so often *eventually* involved and can become a regular and repeated event once it begins.

Getting angry from time to time is a normal and natural response when we feel any sort of threat, whether real or perceived. However, if you find yourself consistently using anger as your go-to emotion, it may be time to talk out the issue with a pastor or counselor.

If you realize you are struggling with rage and your family, co-workers, and friends never know when you are going to explode, then the rationalizing and the "oh, that's just the way I am" must stop. Rage is often accompanied by pride and shame, which makes admitting you have a need very tough. Unaddressed and unattended anger all too often ends in a 9-1-1 call. If someone you love struggles with systemic anger, rage, or bitterness, gracefully talk to them and offer help and support before it is too late.

And "don't sin by letting anger control you." Don't let the sun go down while you are still angry, for anger gives a foothold to the devil. ... Don't use foul or abusive language. Let everything you say be good and helpful, so that your words will be an encouragement to those who hear them. ... Get rid of all bitterness, rage, anger, harsh words, and slander, as well as all types of evil behavior. Instead, be kind to each other, tenderhearted, forgiving one another, just as God through Christ has forgiven you. (Ephesians 4:26–27, 29, 31–32)

The phrase "get rid of" means to pull out by the roots until every trace is gone. An analogy would be to not just mow the weeds, but reach down, pull them completely out, and throw them away. In today's passage, Paul wasn't just making a helpful suggestion, but giving a direct command. Anger can certainly change people's lives; it happens every day in the worst of ways. But pulling it out by the roots can change people in the best of ways.

Father, I ask you today to help me be more kind, tenderhearted, and forgiving toward:

Father, I ask you today to help me get rid of my anger and bitterness toward:

"Heavenly Father, help me to be quick to forgive just like You are with me. Teach me to choose compassion over anger, kindness over rage, and forgiveness over bitterness."

Memory Verse

And "don't sin by letting anger control you." Don't let the sun go down while you are still angry, for anger gives a foothold to the devil.

- Ephesians 4:26–27 -

UNRESOLVED *anger* CAN BECOME THE FUSE *leading* TO AN EXPLOSION OF *rage.*

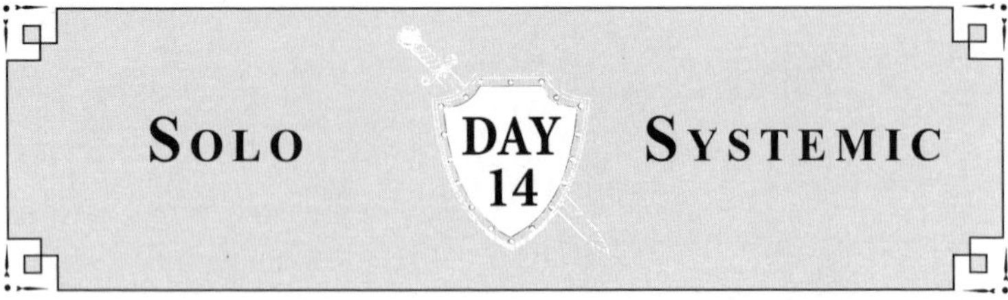

A friend of mine called to ask my advice on an upcoming staff meeting he was leading. As he walked me through his topics to cover, he also went through a list of behaviors he was going to address. After listening carefully, I realized his overarching theme was trying to stop negative attitudes, words, and actions.

When my friend was finished, I inquired, “Are you having trouble with everyone on your team being consistently negative?” He answered, “No, not really. It’s just one person who’s affecting everybody.” My response was, “Why spend money, time, and energy talking to your entire staff when you really just need a face-to-face meeting with one person?”

I went on to share with my friend that from my own experience, I have found that when you challenge a group of people about displaying negativity, the positive people tend to think, *Wow, yeah, I really need to watch that. I can be negative sometimes*. But the negative people will typically think one of two things: *Well, it’s a good thing I don’t have a problem with that*, or *I cannot believe he’s bringing this up again. He needs to let this go. We aren’t negative.*

The reality is positive people are going to respond positively and look inward while the negative people will respond negatively and focus outside themselves. People are driven by where they already are, not where we hope they will go.

So how should we deal with a chronically negative situation, whether an individual or a group? The answer: One person at a time.

By having an honest talk, you may find out a really good reason someone is being negative that you would never have known by generally addressing the issue. This can, in turn, help that person find an answer for a problem and get back to being positive. The best way to help a negative person see how he/she is coming across and affecting any group is to just calmly and gracefully talk to them about it.

To sum up:

> If you have a *systemic* issue, address everyone.
> If you have a *solo* issue, talk to that person and ask how he/she is feeling inside the group. This applies to families, workforce, or anywhere you have a team.

To translate this into parenting, if all the kids are acting up, address all of them. If one child is having an issue, separate him/her from the group and talk privately about what's going on.

All our outward behaviors are driven by internal needs. Negativity is usually a symptom of an unmet emotional desire. Proactively loving people is never going to be the comfortable choice and will always mean doing what's best for the person, not what is easiest for us.

Get the facts at any price, and hold on tightly to all the good sense you can get. (Proverbs 23:23 TLB)

For the Lord gives wisdom; from his mouth come knowledge and understanding. He holds success in store for the upright, he is a shield to those whose walk is blameless, for he guards the course of the just and protects the way of his faithful ones. Then you will understand what is right and just and fair — every good path. For wisdom will enter your heart, and knowledge will be pleasant to your soul. Discretion will protect you, and understanding will guard you. (Proverbs 2:6–11 NIV)

Father, please grow me in Your wisdom and teach me how to positively deal with (person/people):

Father, guide me in how to handle this situation that I have been avoiding:

"Heavenly Father, give me understanding and guidance as to when I need to deal one-on-one for someone's sake and then to have the discretion and strength to know when I need to address any issues with any group."

MEMORY VERSE

GET THE FACTS AT ANY PRICE, AND HOLD ON TIGHTLY TO ALL THE GOOD SENSE YOU CAN GET.

- PROVERBS 23:23 TLB -

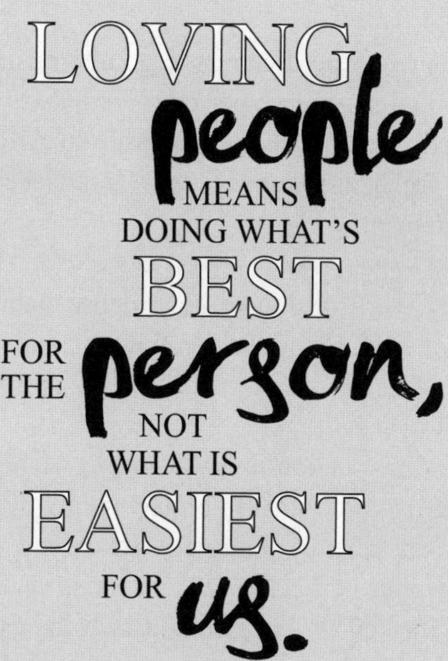
LOVING
people
MEANS
DOING WHAT'S
BEST
FOR THE person,
NOT
WHAT IS
EASIEST
FOR us.

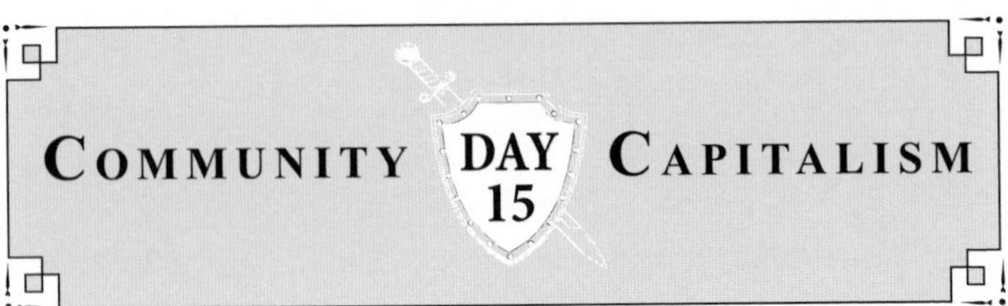

COMMUNITY DAY 15 CAPITALISM

The great entrepreneurial dream is to go into business for yourself, call your own shots, be your own boss, and become a success on your own terms. The pull-yourself-up-by-the-bootstraps mentality can feel really good if you can succeed. This is the essence of capitalism.

While this may work in the world to define achievement, this mindset is not the right mode in the kingdom and community of God.

Years ago, I had a situation in my own life where I could have attempted to do a major ministry project on my own. But I knew someone who was already doing a great work in that area and I also felt he would be open to a partnership. But this was my "problem": If I asked to join him and help his existing efforts, then his name would be on the project. If I raised funds for my part, why shouldn't they just go ahead and give them to him? Even if I helped significantly grow the work, it would just look like he did it all.

Even when we want God to get the glory, we can still struggle with wanting a little credit, right? Well, as so often happens, His

Word has an exact answer for this dilemma.

Do nothing out of selfish ambition or vain conceit. Rather, in humility value others above yourselves, not looking to your own interests but each of you to the interests of the others. In your relationships with one another, have the same mindset as Christ Jesus: Who, being in very nature God, did not consider equality with God something to be used to his own advantage; rather, he made himself nothing by taking the very nature of a servant. (Philippians 2:3–7 NIV)

So there was my answer in black and white. Jesus made Himself what? *Nothing. The nature of a servant.* That's such an incredible counter-human and counter-cultural statement.

In the business world we're not supposed to just re-invent the wheel, but also try to make the best wheel possible to take over the wheel market. Take over and wipe out the competition. That's called capitalism. But Christianity isn't a form of capitalism, at least not the biblical version.

In the kingdom of God, if someone has already invented the wheel and is glorifying God with it, why not just *work together* to make more wheels? That's called community, which is a vital part of Christianity. Exactly what the early Christ followers formed to advance the global body of Christ we live in today.

This business of churches competing for members in the same town, ministries competing for donors, ministers competing for notoriety, all along not cooperating with one another to justify their own existence — that's spiritual capitalism, not biblical community, which only empowers the enemy and keeps the kingdom from looking how it deserves to look today.

When believers line up in Heaven for rewards, it won't be about the most people packed in a pew, the most dollars raised, the biggest building or budget, or the most social media followers. But it will be about how much we served as Paul encouraged in today's passage and Jesus taught in Matthew 25 — whether we fed, clothed, loved, and healed Jesus, who is evidently covertly disguised throughout history as the "least of these."

When we involve ourselves in any Christian community, we must continually ask ourselves two questions: "*What* is this really about?" and *Who* is this really about?" When our answer gets past our name, our credit, our reputation, our church, and our ministry, and finally gets around to Jesus, then we are safe to proceed.

Father, grow me in humility as Your servant and guide me deeper into community and cooperation with other believers by:

Father, I confess I can be competitive and seek the credit when:

"Heavenly Father, help me to do nothing out of selfish ambition or vain conceit. Rather, in humility to value others above myself, not looking to my own interests but to the interests of others."

Memory Verse

In your relationships with one another, have the same mindset as Christ Jesus.

- Philippians 2:5 NIV -

In HEAVEN, what matters MOST is if we fed, CLOTHED, loved, and HEALED Jesus, who is covertly DISGUISED throughout history as the "LEAST of THESE."

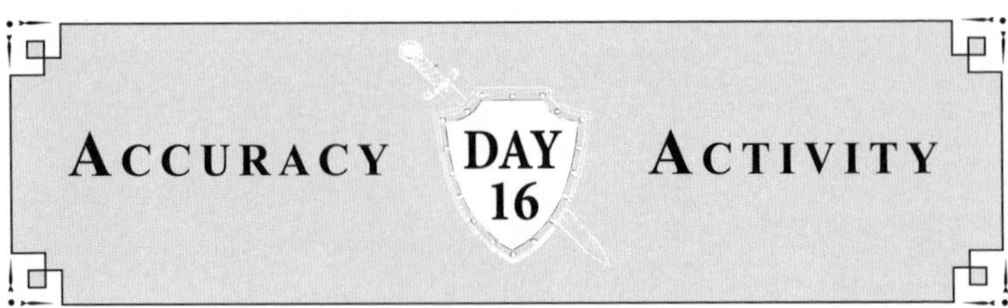

Accuracy Day 16 Activity

For most people today, balancing the busyness in schedules and time management is one of the most challenging and frustrating battles. In no other era in human history has the constant fight to maximize minutes been so exhausting. Looking at the calendar week after week, month after month, even year after year, and not seeing clear results and accomplishments can leave life feeling unfulfilled and at times even meaningless. So many people are busy making constant lateral movements amid endless activity.

While that is the obvious problem, let's take a look at a potential solution by using guns as a simple analogy. (I promise no person or animals will be harmed during this explanation.)

Our culture's approach to time management encourages the use of a "shotgun" loaded with buckshot. Each day we load up our schedules like the 400+ BB's packed inside a shell. We then stand as far back as we can, brace ourselves, pull the trigger, and watch as our best efforts go out as high and wide as possible. Our goal is to increase the likelihood of hitting something — anything — anywhere.

Throughout the day, in person, on our phones, and through social media, we just keep firing in the same forward, general direction. Then we can feel good for a moment when, occasionally, we get several BB's to hit a few targets out there. But with this approach by the end of the day, we feel tired and dissatisfied with the results. When someone asks us how we are doing, the answer is often, "Oh man, so busy. Just slammed. Ready for a break." *Or is it a brake?*

The committed and intentional life of a believer encourages the use of a "sniper rifle." Sit very still and quiet. Listen intently. Factor in all the surrounding elements. Line up the scope. Be patient. Wait for the optimum moment. And then when everything lines up, calmly squeeze the trigger, making your shot count. Focus and faithfulness can bring consistent and confirmed results. Then we move on to the next target on the schedule. We will certainly miss sometimes, but our *accuracy* will definitely increase and become the priority over *activity*.

Throughout the Gospels, we *never* see Jesus huddle up the disciples and say, "Okay, guys, we have so much planned today that we need to get going, so we'll just ask God to bless whatever we decide to do. Now, when I say 'amen,' we're going to split up in all directions and check off the boxes on our ministry list." Never happened. *No, not ever.*

What we do see is Jesus getting regular and specific instructions from the Father. One day was spent healing, another teaching, another feeding five thousand, another casting out demons, and another dealing with the Pharisees in the temple. Throughout the Gospels, we see Jesus constantly allow for "interruptions" to His schedule to deal with the people who approached Him with their needs. Even later when the disciples were sent out two-by-two there were very specific and targeted directions as God revealed His plan.

So if you often feel scattered, full of activity without accuracy, frustrated with no satisfaction, then evaluate your life approach. Could be its time to trade in your "shotgun" for a "sniper rifle." You're going to make a lot less noise but more of your shots will count.

"I tell you the truth, anyone who believes in me will do the same works I have done, and even greater works, because I am going to be with the Father. You can ask for anything in my name, and I will do it, so that the Son can bring glory to the Father. Yes, ask me for anything in my name, and I will do it!" (John 14:12–14)

Father, I ask you to help me balance my time management by:

Father, I confess I waste a lot of precious time by:

"Heavenly Father, teach me to slow down, be intentional with my schedule, focus on what You are doing around me, and make the moments in my life count for You and others."

Memory Verse

You can ask for anything in my name, and I will do it, so that the Son can bring glory to the Father.

- John 14:13 -

Intentionality,
FOCUS,
AND patience,
CAN BRING
IMMEDIATE
AND
CONFIRMED
results.

Following Jesus — Day 17 — Finding Bigfoot

I must confess I have a strange fascination with watching "Bigfoot" shows on TV or "actual footage" clips on YouTube. There's just something intriguing to me about thousands of normal, everyday people all over the world claiming to see giant, hairy creatures who can never be clearly photographed or videoed, much less captured. And no one can even find a skeleton of one that has died.

Whether actual anthropologists or reality TV actors, these Bigfoot researchers travel the globe to search out and analyze any shred of evidence on the mythical creatures. But no matter any episode's plot or location around the world, the endings are always the same. After a solid hour of showing photographs or video footage of a blurry image, talking to eyewitnesses, surveying the locals, and then spending all night in the cold forest with the finest tracking equipment money can buy, no creature is found. At best, they may find another footprint. Sasquatch, Yeti, or whatever name the local folklore has dubbed them, eludes the explorers once again.

So how long have some of these folks been tracking these creatures, seeking the proof for their life's calling? Even though some of them have been at this for over twenty-five years, even still, when you hear them talk and testify of their experiences, they don't speak in "ifs" or "maybes," but certainties. No room for doubt. They. Are. All. In!

Now here's the *real* reason I've been so intrigued by these shows. These folks are totally sold-out that Bigfoot not only exists all over the world, but that the very *next* trip will be the magic moment when they finally find the object of their faith and prove to the world they are not crazy after all. They exhibit an amazing, undeniable, and unquestionable faith. They display a passion and excitement when they speak of their mission, frankly, at a level of which you rarely see today among most Western-culture Christians.

Here's the challenge: Do these explorers display a greater faith in their urban legend than you and I do for our Lord and Savior? The non-believing world around us can easily drive by our churches, listen to our testimonies of faith, and put us in the same category as those who chase Bigfoot. It sounds something like this: "Let me get this straight. You actually believe that an invisible, omniscient Being created the world, then sent His Son to Earth, and now just by believing, you are going to live with Him forever in eternal bliss? Oh, and then there's that part where He may just show up in the clouds one day to take all the true believers home *before* they die." Interesting when we look through a different lens, isn't it?

When you put your feet in the shoes of someone with little to no faith, it doesn't sound that far away from the tale of an elusive giant, hairy, ape-like creature that lives in the forest, does it?

So, as you walk through this lost world, remember three things:

1. People want desperately to put their faith in *something*.
2. Be patient with your non-Christian friends, because to them, your beliefs may sound a little crazy.
3. Let's be sure we're more sold-out about following Jesus than the people who chase Bigfoot.

Now faith is confidence in what we hope for and assurance about what we do not see. (Hebrews 11:1 NIV)

"I have prayed for you, Simon, that your faith may not fail. And when you have turned back, strengthen your brothers." (Jesus in Luke 22:32 NIV)

Father, give me the strength and boldness to share my faith with:

Father, sometimes I get afraid of what people think about my faith because:

"Heavenly Father, help me to never lose sensitivity to those who do not believe in You. Give me Your compassion and care to share what I believe when You open the doors. Increase my faith in what I cannot see — yet."

Memory Verse

Now faith is confidence in what we hope for and assurance about what we do not see.

- Hebrews 11:1 NIV -

Remember—
PEOPLE
TODAY
WANT
desperately
TO PUT THEIR
FAITH
IN something.

Depth DAY 18 Distance

On a call with a friend of many years catching up on life, we discussed how difficult it is today even with the technology to maintain close, transparent relationships amid everyone's busy lives. We talked about the interesting dynamic of how you can meet face-to-face with someone many times and not ever feel like you get past emotional walls or layers of insecurity. Yet you can talk to someone a few times a year on the phone and go deep quickly. What causes such a strange social dynamic? The very nature of that scenario proves that the depths of relationships have little to do with distance. So we must assume that choice is most definitely involved.

How often have we heard or experienced, "Well, after they moved away, things were just never the same between us"? That can even be said when a neighbor just moves across town. Not having the convenience of being able to see someone across the driveway or working out in the yard can literally end a connection. We can decide to not put any work into staying in touch. But "never the same" is a choice we make, just as not truly opening up face-to-face is a choice as well.

For that matter, people living in the same house for years can grow apart and lose touch, while strangers can become close via social media or email in two different countries. Again, it's not about distance but depth.

Here are three encouragements in relationships, our most constantly challenged area of life.

1. While there are certainly situations where God has us be friends with someone for just a season for a specific purpose, we must be sensitive and proactive to maintain the relationships He has for us. No matter the proximity, whether people living in the same house or a once-a-year catch-up phone call across the country, the only way that iron can sharpen iron is for the two blades to engage.

2. Be intentional about constantly growing deeper as a person. Laziness in relationships never makes for deep friendships. Social media posts will never replace genuine care and concern. We certainly see in Scripture how Christ Himself worked daily to deepen His friendships in His circles. Why? Because we are created for *community* and how we grow is *connection*. Christ was the ultimate example of those dynamics. So be deep and go deep. Express your faith. Don't be fearful of a world that needs to see Christ's followers authentically following Him.

3. Is there someone you need to see today? Call? Send an email? Check on? Re-connect with? You might even think it's about you at first, but then discover it's really about them. Someone you know might need a friend right now. Is there anyone you need to go deep with or may need to go deep with you?

To repeat — iron can only sharpen iron when the two blades are engaged. God created us for community, to grow by connection, and change by commitment.

But it was to us that God revealed these things by his Spirit. For his Spirit searches out everything and shows us God's deep secrets.... And we have received God's Spirit (not the world's spirit), so we can know the wonderful things God has freely given us. When we tell you these things, we do not use words that come from human wisdom. Instead, we speak words given to us by the Spirit, using the Spirit's words to explain spiritual truths. ... But we understand these things, for we have the mind of Christ. (1 Corinthians 2:10, 12–13, 16b)

Father, I feel I need to reach out to:

Father, I sometimes struggle in community and connection with:

"Heavenly Father, help me to view all my relationships from my family to my outer circles as connections that You have plans for. Give me the sensitivity and proactivity to be intentional in my actions as I listen to You as my Leader and Navigator."

Memory Verse

And we have received God's Spirit (not the world's spirit), so we can know the wonderful things God has freely given us.

- 1 Corinthians 2:12 -

WE ARE *created* FOR COMMUNITY, *grow* BY *connection*, AND CHANGE BY *commitment.*

Boundaries DAY 19 Barriers

By our sinful human nature, whether we realize it or not, intentional or not, we build barriers. Sometimes hurts have been so bad that people build walls around themselves to keep everyone out. Other times, barriers are built to keep certain people at a distance who we feel have proven to be untrustworthy. When we feel threatened on any level, we can create emotional, mental, and spiritual roadblocks. We decide to "close roads" to keep someone from getting near us.

Certainly there are times when this is right and necessary because a person has caused real harm, but all too often, these are created solely for our own benefit, comfort, and biases. Not for the sake of justice, but from judgment.

As Christ followers, we are to work to *remove barrier*s and keep roads open. The better and more effective work is to *install boundaries* of protection when and where necessary to guard our relationship with God and others. But what's the difference in these two dynamics?

A barrier is anything keeping progress from being made and shrinking our influence. A good offense makes progress by removing barriers, which is exactly why there is a front line between the defense and the quarterback.

A boundary is a line you draw to protect what is inside from what is outside. This is not about restriction and limitation, but freedom and establishing a good defense.

Barriers are all about us. Boundaries are all about our relationship with God and others. Barriers are unhealthy and boundaries support health.

This world has always had dividing lines. Some are created by geography and natural means, while others are invisible and unwritten. When we enter any human organization, one of the first things we must do is figure out where all the lines have been drawn. We then learn them by heart. We separate from each other by economics, race, politics, religion, education, and language, to name a few. We focus more on what divides us than unites us. We are taught at an early age how to disconnect from one another into neat and tidy categories.

But there was One who walked the earth who paid no attention to the boundaries and borders that humans had drawn. In fact, He constantly challenged and battled the limitations man created and enforced to inspire toward finding the personal freedom God offers and intends.

Later, Matthew invited Jesus and his disciples to his home as dinner guests, along with many tax collectors and other disreputable sinners. But when the Pharisees saw this, they asked his disciples, "Why does your teacher eat with such scum?" When Jesus heard this, he said, "Healthy people don't need a doctor — sick people do." Then he added, "Now go and learn the meaning of this Scripture: 'I want you to show mercy, not offer sacrifices.' For I have come to call not those who think they are righteous, but those who know they are sinners." (Matthew 9:10–13)

The Pharisees and teachers of the Law had an issue with Jesus from the moment He stepped foot inside their territory. Why? Because He crossed their boundaries and blew past their borders. He would interact with anyone — Jewish or Gentile, male or female, good or bad, rich or poor, religious or heathen.

When we follow Jesus, we commit to walk where He leads, not tiptoe the tightrope lines drawn by the culture. Representing Christ today, we work to add, not subtract; multiply, not divide, walking across the lines drawn by the world so we can bring His message of hope and grace to everyone, anyone ready to hear. Ephesians 2:14 states, *"For he himself is our peace, ... and has destroyed the barrier, the dividing wall of hostility" (NIV).*

Father, I need to tear down some personal barriers I have built to keep out:

Father, I need to set up some personal boundaries to protect my relationship with You by:

"Heavenly Father, keep showing me where I need to tear down barriers I have built between me and You and others. And please guide me in the places where You want me to place personal boundaries to protect my walk with You to keep me pure."

Memory Verse

"For I have come to call not those who think they are righteous, but those who know they are sinners."

- Matthew 9:13b -

BARRIERS
ARE ALL ABOUT *us.*
BOUNDARIES
ARE ALL ABOUT *our*
RELATIONSHIP
WITH
God AND
OTHERS.

I was asked to be a keynote speaker at an event where several other ministers were invited to share. At the end of one of the sessions, one of the guys in attendance came up and said he needed to talk. He began to open up to me about some deeply personal issues. At the end of the conversation, I asked him why he had singled me out to talk when other capable men were there. He said he could tell I probably had pastoral experience and just sensed I was a safe place. (That detail is important for where he went next in the conversation.)

He then expressed the need for ongoing interaction with someone outside his normal circle for help in the issue he had shared. I told him I would be glad to support him in any way I could. *At his request*, we exchanged cell numbers and email addresses with the understanding there would be future discussions for the purpose of his spiritual growth and moral protection.

A few days later, I sent a brief text asking how he was doing. No response. A few days after that, I sent an email to check on him. No response. A week later, one more try and nothing. Three strikes. Case closed.

What this guy did was what so many people do today. He expressed that he *needed* a deep connection, but what he actually *wanted* was just a session with a priest — a one-time confessional to talk out an issue — to feel good about the purge and move on. Right back into the same issue and struggle until the next talk with someone.

I have had this dynamic happen enough that I gave it a name: "throwing up" — just getting something bad out of your system to stop the emotional nausea. But 99 percent of the time, the sickness quickly returns with a vengeance, because you never actually get rid of the "virus" until you submit to getting real help.

When Christ died on the cross and rose again, He gave us full access to Himself and became our great High Priest. When He gave us the Holy Spirit, He also gave us the authority of His priesthood to become priests ourselves through Him. That's one of the reasons James encouraged us to confess our sins to one another, so that we may be helped and healed through an accountable and grace-filled relationship.

So now that the role of Priest is covered once and for all by and in Christ, what we still desperately need as men are brothers who provide ongoing, keep-it-real, stay-current relationships. Of course there are most certainly times we should meet with a priest, pastor, or professional counselor for help with a deep issue. We must decide to create *conversion* and accountability to change our attitude and behavior, not just meet with someone for a one-time, one-sided *confession.*

And you are living stones that God is building into his spiritual temple. What's more, you are his holy priests. Through the mediation of Jesus Christ, you offer spiritual sacrifices that please God. ... You are royal priests, a holy nation, God's very own possession. As a result, you can show others the goodness of God, for he called you out of the darkness into his wonderful light. (1 Peter 2:5, 9)

Father, thank You for these victories I have experienced through Your grace and help:

Father, here are the places in my life where I tend to just keep confessing but actually need to seek out further help to change:

"Heavenly Father, thank You that I can know You understand my weaknesses and temptations, but also that You trust me as a priest to show Your goodness to others. I pray for more opportunities to change myself while helping and encouraging others in their transformation as well."

Memory Verse

You are royal priests, a holy nation, God's very own possession. As a result, you can show others the goodness of God, for He called you out of the darkness into His wonderful light.

- 1 Peter 2:9 -

When Christ died on the Cross and rose again, He became our High Priest and gave us full access to Himself.

Our work will forever be the answer to the question, "So, *what* do you do?" Everyone assumes that universal "what" refers to one's vocation. But the real question we need to answer for ourselves is "*Why* do I do what I do?"

In the days that God gives us on this earth, He gives us the choice of whether we simply make a living or we actually make a life. Making a living is getting a day's work done to continue our survival. Making a life creates an environment for us to be satisfied in our own souls while also helping others to thrive. While this includes our work, the concept refers to a much bigger picture.

Making a living is typically about doing what someone else expects of us. Making a life is about being whom God has created and called us to be. Making a living will have a point, but making a life has a purpose. Anyone can make a living. In fact, for most of us, other people can learn to do our jobs. But only one person can make your life — you.

Today's passage is longer, but a very important one for us to understand the stewardship aspect of our lives so read carefully.

"Again, the Kingdom of Heaven can be illustrated by the story of a man going into another country, who called together his servants and loaned them money to invest for him while he was gone. He gave $5,000 to one, $2,000 to another, and $1,000 to the last — dividing it in proportion to their abilities — and then left on his trip. The man who received the $5,000 began immediately to buy and sell with it and soon earned another $5,000. The man with $2,000 went right to work, too, and earned another $2,000. But the man who received the $1,000 dug a hole in the ground and hid the money for safekeeping. After a long time their master returned from his trip and called them to him to account for his money. The man to whom he had entrusted the $5,000 brought him $10,000. His master praised him for good work. 'You have been faithful in handling this small amount,' he told him, 'so now I will give you many more responsibilities. Begin the joyous tasks I have assigned to you.' Next came the man who had received the $2,000, with the report, 'Sir, you gave me $2,000 to use, and I have doubled it.' 'Good work,' his master said. 'You are a good and faithful servant. You have been faithful over this small amount, so now I will give you much more.' Then the man with the $1,000 came and said, 'Sir, I knew you were a hard man, and I was afraid you would rob me of what I earned, so I hid your money in the earth and here it is!' But his master replied, 'Wicked man! Lazy slave! Since you knew I would demand your profit, you should at least have put my money into the bank so I could have some interest. Take the money from this man and give it to the man with the $10,000. For the man who uses well what

he is given shall be given more, and he shall have abundance. But from the man who is unfaithful, even what little responsibility he has shall be taken from him." (Matthew 25:14–29 TLB)

We are not really owners of anything, only stewards of life, along with the talents, gifts, skills, and resources hardwired into our DNA. Therefore, God has granted us free will to choose:

- What we do with what He has given
- How much we maximize who we are
- How far we reach, how deep we go
- How faithful we are to Him

Father, I feel my most significant investment in Your kingdom is:

Father, here are the places of my life I am hiding Your gifts and need Your guidance:

"Heavenly Father, I know You had my life mapped out at my conception, so I want to fulfill Your purpose. Help me to daily surrender to Your will so I can be the best steward of each day that You bless me with life."

MEMORY VERSE

FOR THE MAN WHO USES WELL WHAT HE IS GIVEN SHALL BE GIVEN MORE, AND HE SHALL HAVE ABUNDANCE.

- MATTHEW 25:29A TLB -

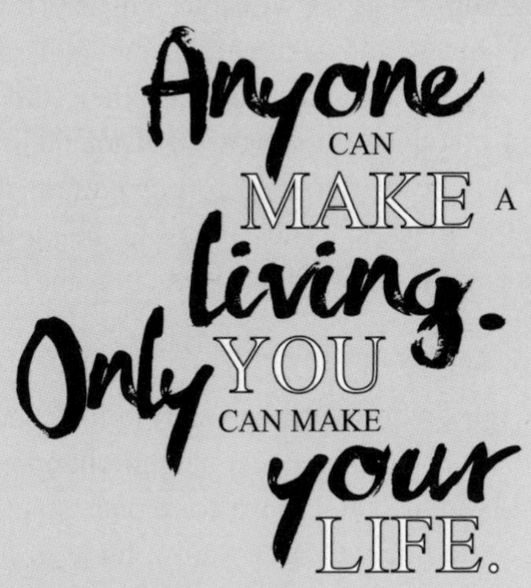
Anyone
CAN
MAKE a
living.
Only YOU
CAN MAKE
your
LIFE.

GRATITUDE DAY 22 GRATIFICATION

One of the ongoing struggles with our sin nature is two-fold: First, we have a tendency to eventually become dissatisfied with the blessings God gives us, and second, we then start to see what others have and convince ourselves we want theirs instead of ours. A saying has been ingrained in our culture for decades: "Keep up with the Joneses." The "Joneses," being the fictitious family who has everything we don't have, becomes our standard for living.

What was once our dream home can start to look second-rate to us compared to those in the newest neighborhood or the house your buddy just bought. The car we were once so excited to get to drive can become one we can't wait to trade in for the latest model. The smartphone that was the ultimate device less than a year ago seems obsolete as we watch the commercials for the new release. The "keep-up" list just goes on and keeps growing.

For decades, marketing and advertising has played off of this constant desire for more and better. And obviously, because companies spend millions each year on ads, the subtle manipulation works. From luxury cars to lavish vacations, from food to fashion, on TV, online, billboards, and in magazines, the parade never stops of the latest, greatest, smarter, and faster things we can't live without.

But looking on the other side of this dynamic, someone somewhere would love to have your job. Your house. Your car. Your talent or skill. Your *whatever*. If you reside in the Western culture, living standards are far above those in the rest of the world. But there's even a likelihood that someone you know might be envious of something in your life.

As Christians, we understand that wanting for ourselves what God has given someone else is a sin called coveting, a subject well covered in the Ten Commandments and also greatly expanded in the Law. God wants us to avoid this practice because it is both selfish and ungrateful at the same time.

So what if we could consistently take the focus off what we want that we don't have — and even accept that we may never get — to look only on our own blessings? To stop our desire for instant gratification and simply be grateful for our own journey that God has entrusted us to walk?

Fighting against our nature and winning can only come about by keeping our eyes on Christ, not on what anyone else has or even what we have. The psalmist offered an amazing prayer in 119:37: *"Turn my eyes from worthless things."* Because the world is constantly screaming its opinions at us, we must allow the Lord to determine what has value for our lives and what is worthless.

The way we can successfully steer clear of God's "do-nots" is to stop being concerned with any perceived lack in our lives and, as basic as it may sound, trust God to give us what He knows we need.

If you love your neighbor as much as you love yourself you will not want to harm or cheat him, or kill him or steal from him. And you won't sin with his wife or want what is his, or do anything else the Ten Commandments say is wrong. All ten are wrapped up in this one, to love your neighbor as you love yourself. (Romans 13:9 TLB)

"So don't worry about these things, saying, 'What will we eat? What will we drink? What will we wear?' These things dominate the thoughts of unbelievers, but your heavenly Father already knows all your needs. Seek the Kingdom of God above all else, and live righteously, and he will give you everything you need. (Matthew 6:31–33)

Father, I want to express my gratitude to you for these blessings in my life:

Father, I confess that I have struggled lately with wanting:

"Heavenly Father, I know all the good things I have in this life come from You and that eternal life is only available as Your gift. Strengthen me to stay in a spirit of gratitude to focus on what I have, not what I don't. Keep my eyes off the 'worthless things' and on You and Your blessings."

Memory Verse

Turn my eyes from worthless things.

- Psalm 119:37 -

FOCUS *only* ON BEING GRATEFUL FOR WHAT YOU *already* HAVE AND WHAT *God* BRINGS INTO YOUR *life.*

Do you ever wake up some days and have an unexplainable sense that everything is going to be great as you experience incredible peace and feel positive about life? But do you also have days that arrive with a sense of doom and dread where hope feels like just a distant memory? Odd that we can have such opposing emotions and such drastically different perspectives while living the very same life, isn't it?

Several years ago on a project where I collaborated with another author, he added "hope" to a list with the nine fruit of the Spirit in Galatians 5. He had come to the conclusion that hope is a crucial virtue offered to us from God in which we can grow just like love, joy, peace, and the other six.

As I began to look at this concept on a deeper level for myself, I realized I often struggle with the biblical version of hope. So I had to ask myself, *Do I really believe when I die I'm going to heaven?* Well, yes. *But on a consistent basis, am I* growing *in the promise of God that life can be full of hope — for eternity* and *today?* And then to dive even deeper: *What is my source of hope? Do I look to the world or any material things? Or is my real focus Christ's presence* in *me as well as* with *me?*

Simply put, more trust in Christ brings more hope in Christ. If we don't truly trust someone, it is difficult to have hope in what they promise. Therefore, a lack of trust reduces hope. But having hope requires some measure of faith. How much I trust God determines my level of hope for life and eternity.

Who wouldn't want more hope today? If hope is like a fruit of the Spirit, then it is not an on-off switch in our lives, dependent on circumstances, but rather a dynamic quality that can grow to be felt, seen, heard, and experienced, not just for ourselves, but also for others. Consider this: Trees don't produce fruit for their own food source. They produce fruit for others to be fed and blessed. God's use of His fruit that He grows in our lives is for us to experience, but also for us to share with others.

What if your hope in Christ became contagious to others? If people around you just felt more hopeful and encouraged after talking with you and being with you? If His work in you was that obvious?

As our culture becomes more and more hopeless, an ever-increasing response from all forms of media is to produce temporary hype over a person or a situation. Hype is simply contrived stimulation to promote or publicize something. Hype has actually become an important aspect of Western religion to convince people to get on board. But when we truly place our hope in anything, we don't require any hype. As we grow in the hope of

Christ, He alone becomes our stimulation to follow, grow, and serve.

We put our hope in the Lord. He is our help and our shield. In him our hearts rejoice, for we trust in his holy name. Let your unfailing love surround us, Lord, for our hope is in you alone. (Psalm 33:20–22)

Therefore, we who have fled to him for refuge can have great confidence as we hold to the hope that lies before us. This hope is a strong and trustworthy anchor for our souls. It leads us through the curtain into God's inner sanctuary. (Hebrews 6:18–19)

Father, my hope and confidence are in You because You have/are:

Father, I confess there are times I look for and rely upon hype in:

"Heavenly Father, understanding today that my hope in You can grow, please strengthen me to trust You more. Then allow my hope to be contagious in a world that desperately needs to see the way out of hopelessness."

Memory Verse

We put our hope in the Lord.
He is our help and our shield.

- Psalm 33:20 -

Stand up for the HOPE you have INSIDE YOU so you won't fall for the HYPE around YOU.

COMMITMENT DAY 24 COMPLIANCE

We all know the definition of commitment quite well. But compliance is a word we should also understand to contrast and know the difference. Both the definition and connotation of compliance means to work to take care of some action. But compliance requires conforming to a requirement or demand where we yield to someone. In fact, often we hear the phrase, "He was forced to comply." Today, we want to take a look at how much we are committing for positive reasons and how much we are just complying to appease others.

Our out-of-control culture's focus on success through an environment of busyness tends to create:

1. Over-promising
2. Over-commitment
3. Under-producing

Do any of these words sound familiar to you? Maybe even make you a bit uncomfortable? Being honest, we are all guilty of these from time to time. The issue is when they become the norm and a vicious cycle begins that we aren't certain how to stop.

So a project or endeavor comes your way and for any number of reasons you feel the pressure to respond with a yes. Even if you are honest and admit you have no desire to take part and/or have the time to carry out the work. Next, the realization comes that there is no way the agreement made is going to be completed, thereby confirming, once again, an over-commitment has taken place. Lastly, completion of the promise and the commitment made is nonexistent. And another regret is added to the list. Unfortunately, we all know what this feels like.

So why does this happen? Here are three possibilities:

1. People-pleasing
2. Fear of conflict
3. Aversion to the truth

Likely, especially if you take the time to go through a book such as this, one of your life goals is to be a man of integrity. An even deeper goal for many is to be a person with a reputation for godliness and following Christ. When we over-promise, over-commit, and under-produce, this not only hurts our name, but His. When we work to please people for the wrong motives, avoid potential conflict at all costs, and passively avoid the truth just to try and "juggle without dropping," we hurt our name — and His.

The practical response might be to make a call or send an email to apologize, get honest, and offer realism on a deadline. Or the consequence may be to just "suck it up" and get through your current commitments, then hit the reset button.

Author and speaker Bob Goff recommends that every Tuesday we should quit something. Why would he suggest this? Because he knows he is speaking to an overcommitted culture that needs to slow down and be realistic about what is possible in life. The best way to stop over-commitment is to learn to quit some things.

We are all going to make mistakes in our day-to-day dealings with people. We are going to mess up and miss something. Today, we are talking about a *pattern* of letting people down, hurting our reputation, and our witness.

The great news is God is quite good at helping us wipe the slate clean, begin again, and walk in a new direction with a fresh outlook, following His lead. In fact, it's one of His specialties.

Let love and faithfulness never leave you; bind them around your neck, write them on the tablet of your heart. Then you will win favor and a good name in the sight of God and man. (Proverbs 3:3–4 NIV)

Father, here are the places I need to get honest and hit the reset button:

Father, these are the places where I am over-promising, over-committing, or under-producing:

"Heavenly Father, help me to constantly come to You for my schedule, to determine my yeses and my nos. Lead me in the demand for my time to allow Your wisdom to manage my life according to Your will."

Memory Verses

Let love and faithfulness never leave you; bind them around your neck, write them on the tablet of your heart. Then you will win favor and a good name in the sight of God and man.

- Proverbs 3:3–4 NIV -

THE BEST way
TO STOP
over-commitment
IS TO
LEARN TO
quit
SOME
things.

In our resume or bio prepared for any professional setting, we naturally work hard to make ourselves appear to be as amazing as possible. That's the point — sell your positives and play down your negatives to try and win the position. A proper resume is of course not a lie or simply a spin on our abilities, but the design of the document is to accentuate our strong points. That's exactly why a good boss or HR person tries to discover any unseen shortcomings and potential weaknesses to balance a glowing resume, knowing we all have them.

But when we sit alone in the quiet and reflect on our lives, we don't read our resume or bio to ourselves because we already know the truth quite well. In fact, the majority of us tend to focus on the negatives and ignore the positives — the anti-resume, if you will. We can tend to regret, second-guess, and beat ourselves up over the wrong things done and said, or the right things missed and ignored.

As sinners, there is generally somewhat of a gap between the public image we present and the private image with which we live 24/7. But most often the truth is actually somewhere in the middle. While we aren't the superheroes that our bios and resumes make us sound like, we also aren't the losers we can paint ourselves to be in our moments of regrets and self-doubt.

That's exactly the reason the disciples are not only great examples to us, but also incredible inspirations who show the transformation that is possible in Christ. Take Jesus' words about Peter for example.

Now I say to you that you are Peter (which means 'rock'), and upon this rock I will build my church, and all the powers of hell will not conquer it. And I will give you the keys of the Kingdom of Heaven. Whatever you forbid on earth will be forbidden in heaven, and whatever you permit on earth will be permitted in heaven." (Matthew 16:18–19)

Just days later and three verses away …
Jesus turned to Peter and said, "Get away from me, Satan! You are a dangerous trap to me. You are seeing things merely from a human point of view, not from God's." (Matthew 16:23)

As Jesus was being falsely tried …
But Peter denied it. "Woman," he said, "I don't even know him!" After a while someone else looked at him and said, "You must be one of them!" "No, man, I'm not!" Peter retorted. About an hour later someone else insisted, "This must be one of them, because he is a Galilean, too." But Peter said, "Man, I don't know what you are talking about." And immediately, while he was still

speaking, the rooster crowed. (Luke 22:57–60)

And then following Jesus' ascension and the Holy Spirit's arrival, there's this …

Then Peter continued preaching for a long time, strongly urging all his listeners, "Save yourselves from this crooked generation!" Those who believed what Peter said were baptized and added to the church that day — about 3,000 in all. (Acts 2:40–41)

While we can't believe our own press, we must also learn to bypass the emotional beat-down we give ourselves. We can choose to view ourselves as Jesus does, through eyes of grace and mercy, accepting the identity He provides us in and through His power. As people of flesh with no righteousness of our own, we're miraculously saved, free to live under submission to the power of the Holy Spirit. Now there's a bio!

Father, here are the qualities people seem to admire that I know You gave me:

Father, here is one private place in my life where I still need Your victory:

"Heavenly Father, You and I know the gap between my public image and my private life. Please guide me and grow me to be the same man everywhere I am, just as You lived when You were here."

Memory Verse

"And I will give you the keys of the Kingdom of Heaven. Whatever you forbid on earth will be forbidden in heaven, and whatever you permit on earth will be permitted in heaven."

- Matthew 16:19 -

A RELATIONSHIP
WITH
Christ
WILL BRING
THE
balance
BETWEEN
OUR
public
AND PRIVATE
lives.

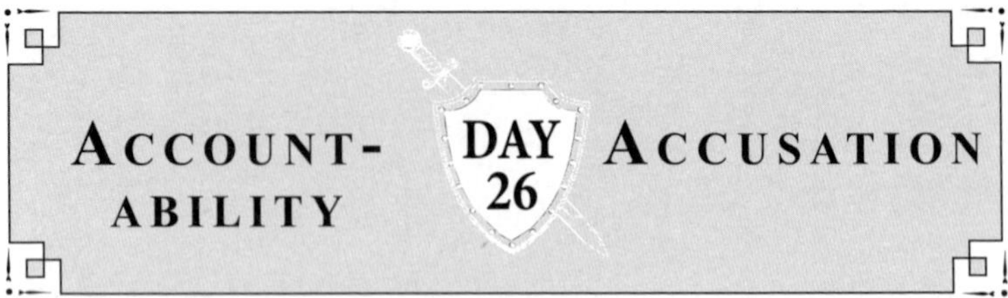

See if you can find the difference in these two sentences:

- Where were you last night between 8:00 and 11:00 p.m.?
- Where were you last night between 8:00 and 11:00 p.m.?

What about these two?

- You've missed two meetings now. Why aren't you coming?
- You've missed two meetings now. Why aren't you coming?

No, you don't need to read them again. It's not a trick. The sentences are identical. The only difference could be in how they are expressed and the motive of the one asking the question. While you can't *read* motive, you can often *hear* it when spoken to you. We pick up on verbal communication and nonverbal cues and coupled with the relationship, or lack of one, this can trigger what the speaker's intentions might be.

Let's look at the questions above this way. The first sentence in both examples is asked out of accusation with this scenario: I have some information or cause for concern about you. I suspect you may be guilty of something. I think you might be lying to me. I ask the question, assuming wrongdoing, but looking for the truth. I'm accusing you until you prove otherwise. You could most likely hear all that inference in the way I asked you the question.

Even when the person is innocent, the threat of accusation can create defensiveness, anger, and evasiveness in almost anyone. If there is any level of guilt of the issue, then that is where hiding, condemnation, shame, more lies, and so on can deepen.

Let's say the second sentence in both examples is asked out of concern and accountability. Here's the scenario: We have agreed on a transparent relationship with a desire to be open and get healthy together. So I ask the question — after being invited and given permission from you. I inquire out of a heart of protection. While we can lie to one another, the relationship is built around truth and honor for each other's best. I'm assuming you want to do the right thing. And even when a failure occurs, we confess, get it right, ask forgiveness, and move on.

A very different motive, purpose, and outcome occur even when the exact same question was asked. In light of these examples and explanations, consider these statements:

Accountability	Accusation
Based on health	Based on dysfunction
Enters through the front door	Comes in the back door
Proactive	Retroactive
Moves us forward	Sets us back
Designed for growth	Designed for guilt

The Enemy wants us to believe that accountability is squelching or limiting our freedom. Yet all the way back to the garden we see that is a lie. Accountability sets us free to accelerate growth in God's grace. Like a train must have the tracks to speed across the country, accountability offers the necessary path for the most progress in our spiritual growth.

Then I heard a loud voice shouting across the heavens, "It has come at last — salvation and power and the Kingdom of our God, and the authority of his Christ. For the accuser of our brothers and sisters has been thrown down to earth — the one who accuses them before our God day and night. And they have defeated him by the blood of the Lamb and by their testimony. And they did not love their lives so much that they were afraid to die. (Revelation 12:10–11)

Admit your faults to one another and pray for each other so that you may be healed. The earnest prayer of a righteous man has great power and wonderful results. (James 5:16 TLB)

Father, here are my places of true accountability for my growth and protection:

Father, here are the places in my life I can quickly feel accused and struggle with guilt:

"Heavenly Father, thank You that You want to remove all guilt and shame from my life. Forgive me when I allow myself or others to condemn me when You have set me free. Lead me into the right accountable relationships for my growth and protection as I work to help others toward freedom."

Memory Verse

And they have defeated him by the blood of the Lamb and by their testimony.

- Revelation 12:11a -

Accountability sets us FREE to accelerate GROWTH in God's GRACE.

Having had two sons graduate from college, I have heard my fair share of compliments and complaints about professors. One night at dinner, our younger son was telling us about his current semester's classes and teachers. For one particular course, he described a very proactive and engaging professor, one highly rated by students whose classes were always full with strong attendance. As a result of this teacher's obvious passion and skill in their field of study, my son was involved, engrossed, and making connection with the subject. Week in and week out, he could always tell us exactly what he was learning from that professor.

But he had another class that same semester where the teacher taught strictly by the book and lectured in a monotone with the goal of just offering the necessary information to get another class in and out. That professor had low ratings from students for many years and everyone took his class only if they had to. As you might suspect, my son was not interested, not engaged, and couldn't wait to get that subject behind him. And in contrast to the other teacher, he could never tell us much about what he was learning during any given week.

Do you see the connection or, maybe better said, the disconnection? One environment was contagious while the other was clinical. Same place. Same setting. Same potential with a very different outcome.

These days, committed and skilled teachers certainly don't guarantee 100 percent engaged students, but providing a contagious environment certainly creates a far better opportunity than a clinical one.

Jesus was also a teacher. In fact, he taught so often in public that many called him by the name "Teacher." He could certainly have chosen to drone on and on in a monotone if He had wanted to. As the Creator, Christ could communicate any way or in any style He wanted. He could have stood with authority in the temple and simply read from the Law, if His only goal was to just communicate the rules to mankind.

But instead Jesus desired to create a craving for people to enter God's kingdom. He wrapped His teaching in stories, parables, and even sometimes, cryptic phrases like "easier for a camel to go through the eye of a needle" (Matthew 19:24). People gathered by the thousands to hear Jesus speak for a reason.

Every day, we are teaching people too. We instruct, inform, educate, and communicate with everyone around us, whether we realize it or not. No matter our age, job, position, or status in life, we are teaching someone on a regular basis.

So ask yourself: How would my "students" rate my "class"? What is my own level of engagement with the people around me? Can people not wait to hear from me or, rather, not wait to "get out of my class"?

And the key question to ask today: Is my faith contagious or clinical?

The presence of God's Spirit will create contagion when we get out of the way, connect, and let Him teach *through* our lives by both words and example. Religion promotes a clinical setting but a relationship with Christ creates a contagious environment in which to grow and mature.

When Jesus had finished saying these things, the crowds were amazed at his teaching, for he taught with real authority — quite unlike their teachers of religious law. (Matthew 7:28–29)

But in your hearts revere Christ as Lord. Always be prepared to give an answer to everyone who asks you to give the reason for the hope that you have. But do this with gentleness and respect. (1 Peter 3:15 NIV)

Father, here are the places I feel that my life and faith are contagious:

Father, here are the places in my life where I know I am being clinical and need Your help:

"Lord Jesus, what great examples we have of how You constantly engaged with people on their level, whether it was one woman or thousands of men, whether the Pharisee or the fisherman. Help me to be a contagious follower of Yours."

Memory Verse

But in your hearts revere Christ as Lord. Always be prepared to give an answer to everyone who asks you to give the reason for the hope that you have. But do this with gentleness and respect.

- 1 Peter 3:15 NIV -

Every day, NO MATTER who YOU ARE OR WHAT YOU do, YOU ARE teaching PEOPLE.

Interaction DAY 28 Isolation

In the past five years, would you say your human interaction has decreased, increased, or stayed the same? With the culture constantly gaining speed, encouraging isolation, and relying on social media, most people's influence on their fellow humans is shrinking. Technology is replacing actual personal engagement.

The most interesting dynamic is that this social segregation is not by necessity, but rather by choice. We work to restrict the number of people we actually need to "do life." While we may not ever admit it, we view many in our circles as expendable.

Today, companies "downsizing" can mean decreasing the number of employees needed to produce the same bottom line. "Purging" refers to cutting people from an organization who are deemed unnecessary. We have become accustomed to these terms and dynamics that have trickled down into our personal thinking in so many ways.

Statistics tell us that the average global Facebook user has 338 "friends" with the median number being around 200. But that same typical user if faced with a personal crisis would actually trust only *four* of those people. So only about one to two percent of those who are online "friends" are actually authentic with the potential of regular face-to-face interaction and dependence. The gap between virtual friends and actual friends is widening by the year.

As Christ followers living in this culture, we all must ask ourselves: In any given week, how much eye-to-eye, heart-to-heart ministry is occurring in our lives? That question is not about creating guilt, but simply making an honest evaluation of our *actual* influence and interaction. So how should we respond?

We can commit our intentional efforts to:

- Seek out face-to-face engagement with actual people
- Work to expand our circle of friends
- Pay attention to the people we meet and encounter in person
- Stop and proactively listen to those people
- Ask questions to understand and express concern
- Put away the phone or device in the presence of an actual person

If we are going to truly impact the world for the cause of Christ, this will occur through God's original plan where we as His followers love our neighbors, meaning all those we meet.

Consider this: God gave humans free will upon creation. They then used that free will to disobey Him and side with His enemy.

So to remedy the problem of sin, God sent His Son to die and pay the debt of sin. But then God chose to give the responsibility of sharing His answer back to the very people who created the problem to begin with! That makes no sense to us, but it is exactly what God has done. Entrusted you with His answer for mankind's eternal problem.

So in response to this great act of trust we must choose interaction and come out of isolation. Decide today that you will look for moments to genuinely interact in an unhurried and intentional manner. Just see what God will do to bring blessing in your life and to those around you, through you.

All the believers devoted themselves to the apostles' teaching, and to fellowship, and to sharing in meals (including the Lord's Supper), and to prayer. A deep sense of awe came over them all, and the apostles performed many miraculous signs and wonders. And all the believers met together in one place and shared everything they had. They sold their property and possessions and shared the money with those in need. They worshiped together at the Temple each day, met in homes for the Lord's Supper, and shared their meals with great joy and generosity — all the while praising God and enjoying the goodwill of all the people. And each day the Lord added to their fellowship those who were being saved. (Acts 2:42–47)

Father, give me opportunities this week to interact with:

Father, here are the ways I know I am isolating myself:

"Heavenly Father, I believe You have the perfect plan laid out for me and know whose lives I am supposed to touch in Your name. Lead me out of isolation and into the interactions You have for me. Show me with whom I need to share my life and Your life."

Memory Verse

All the believers devoted themselves to the apostles' teaching, and to fellowship, and to sharing in meals (including the Lord's Supper), and to prayer.

- Acts 2:42 -

CHOOSE *interaction* AND COME OUT OF *isolation.*

Personal Check — Day 29 — Gift Card

Let's say it's your birthday and a friend gives you an envelope. You open it to find a gift card inside. The friend didn't write how much money is on the card, so you know you'll have to go online to find the balance. Because of the relationship, you believe the card has some value, but you have no idea how much until you can check later.

The popularity of giving gift cards is because they are readily available in retail stores and online. They are quick and easy to get but require no attention or imagination to give. Gift cards aren't specifically for anyone, can even be given away for someone else to use, and are generic in nature.

When any of us open our Bibles, we can randomly read through passages out of duty or guilt, because as Christians we are "supposed to read God's Word." This approach to Scripture is a lot like receiving a gift card. We know it has some value but don't really feel its personal to our lives. The Bible is available everywhere and anyone can read it anytime (at least in the Western hemisphere).

Now back to the birthday analogy. What if a family member

hands you a card and inside is a personal check made out to you for $500? You immediately know by looking at it exactly who gave it to you, that it's specifically for you, and exactly the value it has. It is not generic for anyone, but is specific to you. The gift is personal and the value expressed from the giver to you is immediate.

As Christ followers, engaging with our Bibles should be like receiving a personal check. When we find His message for us in His Word, we know through the power of the Holy Spirit speaking to us that God gave it. We know by faith the message is for us and we know exactly the value it has in our lives. The gift is personal and the value expressed from the Giver is immediate.

What is the real difference in this gift card and personal check example? Two things: Expectation and attitude.

The gift card represents religion. The personal check represents a relationship.

Every day, God writes a "personal check" to each of us in the form of a message from His Word. His eternal truth comes to meet our needs and desires for the day and He speaks inside very intimate words to provide an invaluable gift for us.

Another analogy, which is not original to me, is receiving junk mail versus a love letter. One is scanned and tossed, because it means little or nothing. The other is targeted for the heart and is personal. One is barely read, while the other is scoped over and over in detail.

So do you want to read junk mail or a love letter? Do you want a gift card or a personal check? God has already promised which one He will deliver today. The choice of what you receive from Him is up to you.

For the word of God is alive and powerful. It is sharper than the sharpest two-edged sword, cutting between soul and spirit, between joint and marrow. It exposes our innermost thoughts and desires. (Hebrews 4:12)

In addition to all of these, hold up the shield of faith to stop the fiery arrows of the devil. Put on salvation as your helmet, and take the sword of the Spirit, which is the word of God. (Ephesians 6:16-17)

Father, my favorite verse/passage that I feel expresses your love and care for me is:

Father, here are the ways I still struggle with reading and receiving Your Word:

"Father, I pray Your Holy Spirit will help me better understand and value Your Word. Give me insight, wisdom, and personal application as I read. Help me to see You in every word. Help me to see my life in every word. Place Your truth in my heart for myself and others."

Memory Verse

Hold up the shield of faith to stop the fiery arrows of the devil. Put on salvation as your helmet, and take the sword of the Spirit, which is the word of God.

- Ephesians 6:16-17 -

Every day God writes a "personal check" in the form of a message from His Word.

1 Samuel 15:22 states:
"What is more pleasing to the LORD: your burnt offerings and sacrifices or your obedience to his voice? Listen! Obedience is better than sacrifice, and submission is better than offering the fat of rams."

Then Samuel said, Do you think all GOD wants are sacrifices — empty rituals just for show? He wants you to listen to him! Plain listening is the thing, not staging a lavish religious production. (MSG)

Too often in my own life, I have found myself sacrificing when I should be obeying — doing what I decided was my best *service* for God when I should have been *submitting* to Him. And then far too often, the sacrifice becomes more about me than the Lord. More about what I want to do *for* Him *in* His name than what He wants me to experience *with* Him *because* of His name. Being honest, in those times I can easily start to think, *Hey, God! Hey, everyone! Look at my sacrifice*.

But I need to wait on Him to speak rather than just going to work on my own. Mere spiritual busyness does not equal obedience.

Even church activity can become a constant sacrifice when we aren't allowing God to direct the ministry.

When we think, *What am I going to do? What will "fix" this situation?* we are, in essence, asking, "How can I make a sacrifice to take care of this on my own?" As Christ followers, we should be asking, "God, what do You want here? Have You already provided the sacrifice? How can I obey You?"

As busy, do-it-yourself, get-it-done, mark-it-off-the-list people, we can become accustomed to "laying down our lives" for family, job, church, and countless situations that are indeed "good." But we can end up training ourselves to sacrifice before we even consider what might be the correct steps of obedience. We make assumptions and take action before consulting God. Or we altogether miss the fact that He has already provided.

Years ago, I had a man ask to meet with me because he knew I had experience with starting and maintaining various ministries. He shared his strong desire and sense of calling to start a specific work and then began to talk about the need for funding and raising money. He also expressed his hesitancy about seeking out support since he had never done anything like that before.

When he was done, I asked him if he had received any unexpected financial blessings in the recent past. He responded that a close relative had died a few years back and left him a sizable amount of money. I then asked him, "Could it be that God provided the money for your ministry before He ever gave you the call? Maybe His plans for that provision are different than what You are thinking. Maybe He already answered your prayers." The look on his face told me the dots suddenly connected. The sacrifice had already been made. The provision had been given. Nothing but obedience to the calling was now required.

There are so many times in all our lives when the sacrifice of Christ has already covered us, giving the opportunity to simply submit and move into what He has waiting for us. Applying this 1 Samuel 15:22 principle, we:

- Wait on Him; don't start worrying about what to do.
- Watch for Him; stay alert and look for what only God can do.
- Worship Him; focus on God and don't go to work on your own solution.
- Work with Him; when He does invite you to His work, simply obey.

Where are you sacrificing when you should be obeying? Once you answer the question, stop and listen to His voice.

Father, here are the places I feel I am submitted and obedient to You right now:

Father, here are the places I am striving and sacrificing when I need to surrender to You:

"Father, teach me the balance of obedience and sacrifice. Empower me to wait on You, watch for Your activity in my life, worship as I wait, and then go to work only when and where You lead."

Memory Verse

"What is more pleasing to the Lord: your burnt offerings and sacrifices or your obedience to his voice? Listen! Obedience is better than sacrifice, and submission is better than offering the fat of rams."

- 1 Samuel 15:22 -

WAIT. Watch.
WORSHIP. Work.

PHYSICAL DAY 31 DIGITAL

"Digital footprint" is one of the many new phrases created in this generation that didn't exist up until a few years ago. The term refers to the "trail" we leave of our evidence and history of web searches, websites visited, social media surfing, and any other online activity. But of course, this is not at all like a physical impression that can be swept or wiped away. No matter what steps you take or how many days pass, this footprint will remain, stored away in the chips and servers, even when computer history is "deleted."

The digital footprint is how the sidebar ads magically remind you of that book you looked at on Amazon last night or the summer vacation you priced last week on Expedia. This is how the authorities catch online criminals and how attorneys provide much of the evidence offered today in trials from divorces to prosecutions.

The digital footprint for any of us reveals a lot. Where we go online. How much we're online. For many people today, especially those who are posting on social media, they are literally leaving a trackable history of what they've done, where they've gone, who they've been with, where they've eaten, and what they think, believe, and have said about life. From work to wishes, searching to shopping, habits to hobbies, all are on display for anyone to see. For a people who increasingly demand so much privacy, we have voluntarily become a very public society.

But let's consider another print we leave in life, one that also often goes unseen yet will never go away: the Jesus handprint.

This is created forever when we touch someone's life in His name by offering a:

- Word of encouragement
- Helping hand
- Listening ear
- Prayer for strength
- Financial gift
- Witness of the Gospel

The Jesus handprint reveals a lot about us too — how much we love Him and how much we love our neighbors. Depth and devotion, faith and focus, care and commitment all displayed. The Jesus handprint might be seen by some here on Earth, but will certainly be viewed clearly in eternity. In fact, in the end, this will be the only earthly thing that counts in Heaven.

One day, our digital footprint will finally fade away, megabyte by megabyte disappearing under layers of new data. But our Jesus handprint never will. And the irony is our focus on Jesus will take care of the digital footprint — and any other past, present, or future impression.

Today, where can you leave the handprints of Jesus?

"Then the King will say to those on his right, 'Come, you who are blessed by my Father, inherit the Kingdom prepared for you from the creation of the world. For I was hungry, and you fed me. I was thirsty, and you gave me a drink. I was a stranger, and you invited me into your home. I was naked, and you gave me clothing. I was sick, and you cared for me. I was in prison, and you visited me.' Then these righteous ones will reply, 'Lord, when did we ever see you hungry and feed you? Or thirsty and give you something to drink? Or a stranger and show you hospitality? Or naked and give you clothing? When did we ever see you sick or in prison and visit you?' And the King will say, 'I tell you the truth, when you did it to one of the least of these my brothers and sisters, you were doing it to me!'" (Matthew 25:34–40)

Father, lately my Jesus handprint has been focused on reaching:

Father, here are the ways I am spending too much time online or in the wrong places and need Your help:

"Father, I realize one day when I stand before You that my phone, tablet, laptop and all I did online will have little to do with what I have done for You. Impress on me and make me bolder to place my time and energy in what will count for You in eternity."

Memory Verse

And the King will say, "I tell you the truth, when you did it to one of the least of these my brothers and sisters, you were doing it to me!"

- Matthew 25:40 -

KEEP Jesus
MORE
important
THAN YOUR
SMARTPHONE.

Treasure DAY 32 Trash

Financial experts report that one of the most lucrative investments a person can make today to create virtually risk-free, secure, ongoing monthly income year in and year out is to build storage units almost anywhere in the United States. From metropolitan cities to rural towns, Americans like to keep their stuff. When the closets are full, the attic is full, and the garage is full, then a storage unit is next to take the things we don't use anymore and yet still can't seem to live without.

I once talked with a man who makes his living running his own storage business. He told me it is not unusual at all for someone to walk in, rent a unit, hand over their credit card number for the monthly charge, move in their stuff, and he never sees them again until years later. The only contact he may have with them is if their card fails to charge. He said that many of his renters could have hauled everything they put in storage to the dump and saved thousands of dollars. But of course he's glad they didn't. The old saying goes, "One man's trash is another man's treasure," and the storage business brings new meaning to those words.

Throughout the course of every single day, we all produce trash — unwanted, unused stuff we no longer need or will use. If we live a day, we produce trash in that day. This is a given.

But there is another kind of trash that we produce every day. It can be a self-centered attitude, an unfair criticism we spew out, a damaging habit we engage in again, someone who we put off who shouldn't be, or someone we entertain who we shouldn't. Each day, we produce that kind of garbage as well.

Our treasure is obviously the highly valuable things in our lives that we need and want. But like the internal trash we can produce, we have the same opportunity to produce an intangible treasure. For Christ followers, these are the fruit of the Spirit; the gifts of the Spirit; and the attitude, words, and actions from a mind being transformed by Christ. This is the new life God brings as we express His love and grace to our neighbors.

One of the great frustrations of the human existence is how easy it is, so often without even thinking, to produce trash, while treasure seems to come only through targeted and intentional commitment. This is exactly why obedience and submission is so important.

Trash comes easy; treasure requires work.

Today, maybe it's still early and you haven't produced a single piece of trash yet. But it's also a new day where you most certainly can produce treasure — something not just valuable to you, but maybe even more so to the people around you.

The great news of the Gospel is our trash can be forgiven, so God's treasure can be given.

Teach those who are rich in this world not to be proud and not to trust in their money, which is so unreliable. Their trust should be in God, who richly gives us all we need for our enjoyment. Tell them to use their money to do good. They should be rich in good works and generous to those in need, always being ready to share with others. By doing this they will be storing up their treasure as a good foundation for the future so that they may experience true life. (1 Timothy 6:17–19)

Father, I believe the greatest treasure I have from You is my:

Father, here are the places I struggle with producing and collecting trash and need Your help to throw out:

"Father, the Scriptures are clear that Your idea of treasure is very different from the world. In fact, we cannot buy what You place the most value upon. Please help me to keep handing my trash over to You, not holding onto it, and allowing You to transform my life into Your treasure."

Memory Verse

Tell them to use their money to do good. They should be rich in good works and generous to those in need, always being ready to share with others.

- 1 Timothy 6:18 -

THE
GREAT news
OF THE
GOSPEL
IS OUR
trash
CAN BE
FORGIVEN,
SO God's
TREASURE
CAN BE
given.

Speak Up — Day 33 — Shut Up

When should I speak up? When do I need to shut up? Some of the biggest problems we create in our lives involve the proper use of our speech. Speaking when we shouldn't, and not speaking when we should, can create major issues in our communication. Ironically, we can get in just as much trouble and hurt someone just as badly by what we *don't* say as opposed to what we *do* say. The question of, "Why did you say that?" versus "Why didn't you say something?" can be just as difficult.

As men, regardless of our personality type, in our immature days we could tend to "speak first and ask questions later." I have a good friend whose wife jokingly tells him, "When it comes to your mouth, your method is 'ready, fire, aim.'" But as humans, we are all guilty of this approach at times.

I was once talking with a friend about a meeting he was in where people inside their organization were clearing the air on some conflicts. He said the one guy in the room who everyone knew had the most issues with the staff and consistently mouthed off, was the quietest during the meeting. He avoided the very opportunity to try to find resolve when his speech could matter most.

So what causes us to speak up when we shouldn't and shut up when we shouldn't? Here are three thoughts for this ongoing battle in us all:

1. **Listen more.**

   Not *hear* more but *listen* more. Hearing someone speak and listening to what they say are two very different things. Active listening is a skill that we must constantly work on and hone, especially in our very noisy culture. For introverts, this means taking in what is said and then being proactive to respond. For extraverts, this may mean taking a pause, closing the mouth, and opening the ears.

2. **Make your words count.**

   Not *count* your words but *make* them count. When you speak, know that your words matter to you and the other person. Many of us need to cut the fluff we build around what we truly need to say. We can nix the preamble speech before we deliver the real point. We see throughout Scripture, particularly in Proverbs, that the wise are not silent; they listen but then say the right thing at the right time in the right way. One of the primary ways we count someone as being wise is because of what they say, how they say it, and the timing and power of their chosen words.

3. Ask Jesus for His ears and mouth.

As the Son of God, Jesus knew exactly the perfect words to speak at all times, in all circumstances. If His Spirit is alive in us, we can access His words and ears. In your communication, pray regularly that you hear people as He would and speak to them as He would. This makes all the difference in how we understand others and how we are understood.

Regardless of our age, personality, background, and life circumstances, we can change our communication for the better. We can continually grow in what we say, what we don't say, and how intently we listen to others. Christ can be Lord over our personalities, our ears, and our mouths.

Everything in me will celebrate when you speak what is right. (Proverbs 23:16)

To those who listen to my teaching, more understanding will be given, and they will have an abundance of knowledge. (Matthew 13:12a)

Father, here are the situations in my life right now where I need the strength to speak up and share truth:

Father, here are the situations in my life right now where I need the wisdom and discretion to be quiet and listen more:

"Father, I know my speech is a constant reflection of my heart so give me wisdom to know when to speak and when to be quiet. Temper my personality with Your Spirit so I can share Your wise words with others."

Memory Verse

Everything in me will celebrate when you speak what is right.

- Proverbs 23:16 -

Christ can be Lord over our personalities, our EARS, and our mouths.

An action is defined as "an act of the will; a thing done; the accomplishment of a thing; the bringing about of an alteration by force." A reaction is defined as "the way someone acts or feels in response to something that happens or is said; resistance or opposition to a force or influence; a response to some treatment, situation, or stimulus." (Merriam-Webster)

We all understand that a reaction is what occurs following an action. The action comes first. Reaction second. Throughout our days, we react to other's words and actions, and even their attitudes, with our responses being all the way from silent thoughts to physical events. Our lives are filled with constant actions of our own and reactions to those around us.

In the various areas of life — marriage, family, work, school, friends, neighbors, church, community — we must evaluate whether our tendency in relationships is to initiate action or respond in reaction. As with so many other areas of our identities, we can write off our choices in how we respond by blaming our personality or our past. But as Christ followers our spiritual maturity and growth must take priority and precedence over any of those personal dynamics. God is continually working to redeem all of who we are, all of the time.

Here are the three elements typically found in those who live primarily by reaction:

1. **Apathy**

   Avoiding action and any potential conflict — real or perceived — and staying in reaction mode is a lack of proactivity. While this approach can also be considered as laziness, apathy is a stronger word because it is an anti-action as in unconcerned, unaffected, or unresponsive. Deciding to consistently lack action in relationships and communication brings about an apathetic attitude.

2. **Fear**

   Consistent lack of action is a sign of fear. Constant reaction just reinforces and creates more fear. The very nature of fear is a reaction to a negative stimulus. When we make a decision to overcome our fears and press onward, we choose action over reaction. Faith, the opposite of fear, always invokes some sort of action, even if only to begin to believe.

3. **Distrust**

   When we live and operate life in reaction mode, we don't trust God and we don't trust ourselves, so therefore we don't trust others. Distrust is a reaction to some sort of past hurt and disappointment where we choose to protect ourselves at all costs. The only way to overcome distrust is to choose the action of trusting once again. While these statements may seem elementary in some ways, we all know how difficult these are to overcome.

Someone who continually lives in reaction mode will eventually see themselves as victims of those around them who take action. A sign of spiritual maturity in any area of life is moving from reaction to action, even if its baby steps, merely crawling in the right direction.

Of course, we cannot possibly live all of life in constant action because there is always give-and-take required in every relational interaction. But evaluating our tendencies toward action or reaction can help us make healthy adjustments that lead toward fulfilled and successful lives. Consider the life of Jesus. His life was marked with action. Even in His most challenging moments when reacting to the Pharisees' constant accusations, He answered the questions, spoke the truth, and moved on.

When someone says, "He or she is a person of action," those words are always spoken in a positive and affirming light.

Yes, just as you can identify a tree by its fruit, so you can identify people by their actions. (Matthew 7:20)

Oh, that my actions would consistently reflect your decrees! (Psalm 119:5)

Father, here are the places where I need Your help to take the right action:

Father, here are the places where I need Your help to stop reacting to others:

"Father, forgive me when I am apathetic, fearful, and distrusting. Point out to me where I am reacting in a way You are not pleased with. I want to be known as a man of action, but only those that You want me to take."

MEMORY VERSE

YES, JUST AS YOU CAN IDENTIFY A TREE BY ITS FRUIT, SO YOU CAN IDENTIFY PEOPLE BY THEIR ACTIONS.

- MATTHEW 7:20 -

A SIGN OF *spiritual* MATURITY IS *moving* FROM REACTION TO *action.*

A person known to be a producer of any kind can be defined as one who regularly creates something of value for others. While certainly a producer of any product or service will benefit from their work, the very nature of what they do is designed to help and support others. A true producer is not seeking to stockpile what they create for themselves. Therefore, anyone who regularly produces also has the constant opportunity to be a giver.

A consumer is one who regularly seeks to receive and take in something of value to use or own. Our understanding is if you are a human, you are constantly consuming on some level. The word "consumer" in the Western culture has come to mean someone who is in a constant cycle of buying and using, using and buying. Consuming doesn't necessarily imply something bad or negative, but we most definitely connect the concept to getting and receiving for personal benefit.

Looking at Scripture as a whole, we are constantly challenged and inspired to be generous producers who consume in unselfish and moderate amounts.

In our marriage, parenting, relationships, friendships, career, work, business, neighborhood, church, ministry, and community efforts, we must continually ask these two questions:

1. Throughout my life, am I focused more on producing or consuming?
2. Throughout my life, am I focused more on giving or getting?

When we honestly evaluate our lives on a heart level, we may find it frightening how often we make decisions based on "What's in this for me?" As sinful people, we can even learn to justify consuming because of how we produce. Case in point: Why does making more money typically also mean we will spend more money? Financial counselors regularly report that from middle class to millionaires, the people in their offices have the same complaint: "I can't live on what I make." The foundation of this human dilemma is based on the balance of producing and consuming.

So what do we do if we discover our motives and goals are completely off-base with someone or in some particular area of life?

We may need to:

- Ask God for forgiveness and a fresh start
- Ask someone for forgiveness and a fresh start
- Put an end to a situation, relationship, or business deal

- Get pastoral help or counseling
- Put some principles in place (develop personal guidelines)
- Create some accountability (set personal boundaries)
- Change some policies (process of decision making)
- Say no to something
- Say yes to something
- Ask God for wisdom and guidance

Challenge yourself daily to produce something valuable and also give away something valuable.

"I am the true grapevine, and my Father is the gardener. He cuts off every branch of mine that doesn't produce fruit, and he prunes the branches that do bear fruit so they will produce even more. You have already been pruned and purified by the message I have given you. Remain in me, and I will remain in you. For a branch cannot produce fruit if it is severed from the vine, and you cannot be fruitful unless you remain in me. Yes, I am the vine; you are the branches. Those who remain in me, and I in them, will produce much fruit. For apart from me you can do nothing." (John 15:1–5)

Father, the places where I am producing and giving right now are:

Father, the places where I am too much of a consumer and too focused on getting is:

"Father, I know without You I can produce nothing of real value, so I yield to Your Spirit to lead me in balancing my consumption versus my production. I want to be a giver, not a getter. I want to produce fruit in myself, gold in the lives of others, and glory for You."

MEMORY VERSE

YES, I AM THE VINE; YOU ARE THE BRANCHES. THOSE WHO REMAIN IN ME, AND I IN THEM, WILL PRODUCE MUCH FRUIT. FOR APART FROM ME YOU CAN DO NOTHING."

- JOHN 15:5 -

TODAY, *produce* SOMETHING *valuable* AND GIVE *something* VALUABLE.

Sniper — Day 36 — Poison

What if you received a registered letter today from the government informing you that CIA intelligence had been passed to them that you were a target of a terrorist plot? The letter states that you will be killed within the week — no matter where you are. There is no hiding. But you do have one choice — how you die.

The first option is to be taken out by sniper — sudden, random, when you least expect it. No warning. No confrontation. No pain. One shot — gone. The second choice is something you drink or eat will be poisoned. You won't know in what or when, but it will be ingested at some point. The poison will be a very slow death, likely quite painful, and you'll be very aware that you are dying.

Which death would you choose?

99.9 percent are going to answer with "sniper." If this is my only choice and it is going to happen, then I choose random, quick, and done. But here's the oddly ironic twist to this bizarre scenario: in real life, 99.9 percent of us choose the poison. Allow me to explain.

In the realm of sin, disobedience, flesh, and choices, we do occasionally hear of "sniper incidents." A deadly sin was not planned. The temptation hadn't been a long-term issue. But out of nowhere the opportunity presented itself, and in a moment of weakness the person gave in and their life was ruined.

But sin as poison is exactly the opposite of the sniper hit. Very slow, this kind of ongoing cycle of temptation can take years to kill. The point of ingestion may not even be remembered any longer, but the awareness that it's inside you is glaringly evident.

Poison can be anger, bitterness, hatred, jealousy, greed, materialism, apathy, complacency, lust, gluttony, materialism, lying, criticism, blame, laziness, entitlement, betrayal, and on and on. Poison typically starts very small, usually with an event connected to a feeling or an emotion. If not addressed, and especially when entertained, the problem starts to grow. Poison can stay hidden for a very long time, but will always eventually begin to show its effects. And, untreated, it will kill. And possibly even spread to others.

While there will be a few folks taken out by sniper fire, we all have poison flowing through our veins. It will take its sweet time to destroy us, looking for opportunities to manifest symptoms and grow. And we also know the name of the poison in us right now.

The good news is Jesus knows the poison is there, where it is, how much is present, and He holds the cure. The depth of our healing just depends on our level of obedience. Christ has grace, mercy, provision, and deliverance for us, but we have the choice as to how much we accept His cure. Each day, we must decide between the poison and the Cure, the flesh and Spirit, sin and victory. Our salvation is not up to us to gain, it is a free gift of God, but our level of healing and growth lies in our daily decisions to choose Him, to take up our cross that is provided by His mercy, and follow Him.

But now that you've found you don't have to listen to sin tell you what to do, and have discovered the delight of listening to God telling you, what a surprise! A whole, healed, put-together life right now, with more and more of life on the way! Work hard for sin your whole life and your pension is death. But God's gift is real life, eternal life, delivered by Jesus, our Master. (Romans 6:22-23 MSG)

Father, thank You for these places from my past where I know You have brought me healing:

Father, here is the one place I know there is poison still inside that could hurt me and others:

"Father, thank You that You came here and understand the struggle of temptation, yet You endured and defeated sin. Give me the humility and the boldness to continually confess and allow You to be my strength and my hope to defeat the poison in my own life."

Memory Verse

But now that you've found you don't have to listen to sin tell you what to do, and have discovered the delight of listening to God telling you, what a surprise! A whole, healed, put-together life right now, with more and more of life on the way!

- Romans 6:22 MSG -

Christ has GRACE, mercy, PROVISION, and healing for US, but WE have the choice as to HOW MUCH we accept His CURE.

Authentic Auto-tune

Day 37

Regardless of your interest level in music, you have likely heard the word "auto-tune." This is a computer program that can fix pitch variations in the human voice to make a vocal performance sound "perfect." Today, the vast majority of recording artists use this "tool" in recording on some level. There are a few who are regularly pitch challenged that also have to take auto-tune on the road to use in live performances. Their fans have come to expect an exact re-creation of the record, which now can only be performed with the use of technology. So for some artists, you are not actually hearing their real voice anywhere.

Years ago when I was in a Christian band that toured full-time, we also recorded and released records. In that day, nothing like auto-tune existed. We had to work really hard take after take to nail a solid vocal performance. As a result, there were days when due to time and money we had to say, "That's the best we can do. Let's move on." One of the factors that helped this decision was no one in the record buying world at that time was expecting perfection but simply wanting to hear an artist's work.

At the point where I began to produce other artists, I can still remember well sitting in the engineer's booth, listening to a very talented singer who I was helping make the best record possible for the money. The lights in the vocal room were down low with the singer completely in the zone, feeling every note and every moment of the song. The artist's heart and soul would flow out of their mouth, through the microphone, and be captured in the recording.

When the take was over, they would say what every professional singer says, "Let me try it one more time. I can do better." To which the engineer and I would often say, "No! That was absolute magic. There is no way. Your performance was special, anointed, and beautiful." Was it perfect? No. Did they nail every note? No. But did it create emotion in us that made us feel like we just heard something amazing from an artist who has something special to say? Yes, absolutely. That is the goal of all great music; the very reason art exists in the first place. We were after authentic. Not a grand perfection but a captured performance from the heart.

Never before in history has appearance been so important to a culture. With the ever-growing prevalence of social media and the ability to offer our existence through carefully selected filters, what is presented is all too often just "auto-tuned" lives.

But as human beings, we are not auto-*anything*. And deep within our hearts, we all know the truth. So as Christ followers the lost and hurting world around us doesn't need to see our social media-perfected, filtered-picture, utopian, "auto-tuned" lives. But rather, authentic and real expressions of what a flawed and blemished human being looks like when surrendered into the heart and hands of a Perfect God.

For God, who said, "Let there be light in the darkness," has made this light shine in our hearts so we could know the glory of God that is seen in the face of Jesus Christ. We now have this light shining in our hearts, but we ourselves are like fragile clay jars containing this great treasure. This makes it clear that our great power is from God, not from ourselves. (2 Corinthians 4:6-7)

Father, the places I know I must allow myself to be authentic are:

Father, the places where I still struggle and strive to look "perfect" are:

"Father, the very definition of authentic can only be found in total surrender to You. Please take this "fragile jar of clay" and let Your light shine and Your great power pour from my life."

Memory Verse

We now have this light shining in our hearts, but we ourselves are like fragile clay jars containing this great treasure. This makes it clear that our great power is from God, not from ourselves.

- 2 Corinthians 4:7 -

The World longs to see what a flawed and blemished human being looks like when surrendered into the heart and hands of a perfect God.

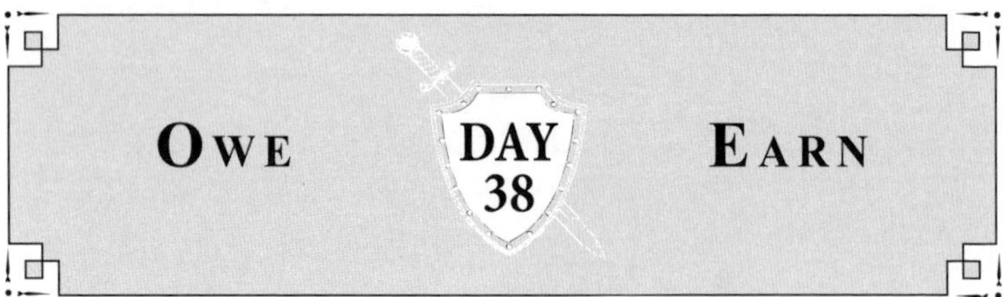

If you have a friend or an acquaintance who is constantly trying to do and say things to win your approval and earn your friendship, how do you feel about that person? If what they say to you or their efforts always feel a bit "over the top" or that they are working too hard to be friends, that's always an awkward spot to be in.

But if you have another friend who regularly affirms you very sincerely and does things to express appreciation for your friendship, how do you feel? Usually, we are grateful for those folks and consider them good friends in our inner circle.

Now the words spoken and the actions taken by both of these people might sound and look very much the same, right? Why is it that one person complimenting you can feel very intrusive while another feels appreciated? Why does one person insisting on buying you lunch feel like a burden while another feels like a kind gesture? Why does one feel like a sad effort to earn your approval and the other like a token of appreciation for the friendship?

Most often, the bottom line for the answer comes down to the motive of the person. We can have a sense of when people are doing things for the wrong reasons versus the right reasons. We can tell when someone has an ulterior motive versus when someone is just being a good friend. In these types of circumstances, our spirits can pick up on verbal and nonverbal cues to know if the interaction is about us or the other person; they can be self-centered or selfless.

Let's apply this concept to our relationship with God. In our prayers and interactions with Him, do we obey to try and win His approval, earn His love? Or seek Him simply out of gratitude for the relationship? Are we motivated to try and get God to meet our desires or are we walking with Him because we love Him?

These two responses can look very much the same as well, right? Yes. So therefore, our "good works" come down to motive too. But who can really tell the difference? Well, at least in your own life, you can. You really do know.

If you believe salvation is a free gift from God and you can do nothing to earn His approval and love, then working to earn it is pointless, tiring, and futile. Much like working two jobs to save up for a car that is already sitting in the garage, bought and paid for. Why work so hard to get something you already have and could never earn anyway?

So the best motive for us is obedience to God practiced out of gratitude. Desiring to please the Giver, using His gifts for exactly what they were intended in the first place.

In your relationship with God, do you try to earn love *from* Him or feel you owe love *to* Him? One is about us never being enough and the other is living with the understanding that God is always not just enough but always more than we need.

Jesus replied, "I tell you the truth, you want to be with me because I fed you, not because you understood the miraculous signs. But don't be so concerned about perishable things like food. Spend your energy seeking the eternal life that the Son of Man can give you. For God the Father has given me the seal of his approval." They replied, "We want to perform God's works, too. What should we do?" Jesus told them, "This is the only work God wants from you: Believe in the one he has sent." (John 6:26–29)

Father, today I am grateful for Your grace and mercy in my life because:

Father, sometimes I feel like I have to earn Your approval because:

"Father, forgive me when I fall back on works and the idea that I earn anything from You. Thank You that the only 'work' You want from me is to believe in You. Thank You for Your free gift of salvation, Your grace and mercy that You constantly pour into my life."

MEMORY VERSE

JESUS TOLD THEM, "THIS IS THE ONLY WORK GOD WANTS FROM YOU: BELIEVE IN THE ONE HE HAS SENT."

- JOHN 6:29 -

AS *His* CHILD,
YOU
already
HAVE
GOD'S
seal
OF APPROVAL.

Investing DAY 39 Wasting

I had a conversation with a friend of mine who is a self-employed entrepreneur. He was telling me about the many meetings he has to set up to try and produce business. Often the person he is meeting with seems very serious and wants to involve him in a project, but then my friend will schedule another meeting according to the other person's demand and calendar. But after spending hours, days, or at times even a couple of weeks, nothing materializes. My friend invested a great deal of time and energy only to find the effort was completely wasted.

But he also said there are the people who, after just one or two meetings, get serious, push the button, lay the money on the table, and he's on his way to creating something important.

So the big question is how do you know the difference between these two early on? Where do you draw the line and where do you show faith and press on?

While this example is of course a business situation, the principle here applies to all stewardship of time because with every moment of every day we are either investing or wasting. There's no neutral zone. Even when we sit and do nothing, we can be wasting time being lazy or we could be investing in rest for our bodies and souls.

For all of our jobs, if someone is paying us to show up and do work, they are entrusting us to invest time and energy in the agreed endeavor. So evaluating our time management through this filter of investment is important.

When it comes to time, God makes no one rich or poor. We're all on equal ground. The abundant life in Christ invites us to invest as much as possible and waste as little as possible.

Are you tired, exhausted, worn out, and whipped? If yes, maybe it's because there is too much wasted time and your heart, mind, and spirit know the truth. If so, what needs to change? What lines need to be drawn? Who do you need to get honest with?

Where are you excited, pumped, and passionate about something? Those feelings are there because you're investing and you see the win.

Consider these questions to evaluate:

- Where am I investing in a person, a project, or a passion?
- In this investment, where and when is someone going to win with what I am bringing to the table?
- Where am I wasting time, energy, and money (my own or

someone else's) and no one is going to win?

A great exercise that actually doesn't take very long to do, is to make a list of what is taking up your time. Just writing everything down and honestly looking at the list can help you make some tough decisions about anything that must go versus something that may need to be added. A periodic honest evaluation of your time can quickly determine where you are investing versus wasting. A second aspect of that exercise is once you write your list, then offer it to God and ask Him to help you discern what is right for you and what is not.

For everything there is a season, a time for every activity under heaven. A time to be born and a time to die. A time to plant and a time to harvest. A time to kill and a time to heal. A time to tear down and a time to build up. ... A time to embrace and a time to turn away. A time to search and a time to quit searching. A time to keep and a time to throw away. (Ecclesiastes 3:1–3, 5b–6)

Father, the one thing I am the most passionate about in my life right now is:

Father, the one place I know I am wasting my resources right now is:

"Father, give me the boldness and the courage to press into the passion You have given me and an equal measure of boldness and courage to stop where I am wasting what You have given."

Memory Verse

A time to embrace and a time to turn away.
A time to search and a time to quit searching.
A time to keep and a time to throw away.

- Ecclesiastes 3:5b–6 -

Invest
IN YOUR
GOD-GIVEN
passion.

Transforming Training

Day 40

I watched legendary animal expert Jack Hanna interview an elephant caretaker and trainer who worked in an African wildlife preserve. The animals in the man's care obviously had mastered several basic commands from verbal and physical cues, all given with great respect and care. When Jack asked about the elephant's ability to be trained, the man answered, "They're extremely intelligent animals so they catch on quickly to any training." The man paused and then smiled as he added, "But it's the relationship that takes time."

I have been in various roles of ministry for forty years and I have seen, regardless of the generation, you can quickly teach any Christian what to *do* — read and study the Word, pray, worship, engage in a small group, share their testimony, serve people, etc. But it's the *be* — how to develop an intimate and authentic relationship with Jesus — that takes time.

Some of the most difficult passages of Scripture are when Jesus teaches that just because we do things in His name doesn't mean entry into Heaven. In Matthew 7, He tells the disciples that on judgment day there will be those who say they have prophesied in His name, cast out demons, and even performed miracles.

But He closes with the harsh truth (paraphrasing): "Get away from Me. Just because You were trained and did spiritual activity doesn't mean You have a relationship with Me."

In an interview, country music icon Garth Brooks was answering a journalist's question about what his typical day on tour looks like. Garth shared that as often as possible, he takes time out in the particular city in which he is performing to work with at-risk kids. When asked why he prioritized this time on the road, he answered, "It's the most important work I've ever gotten to *do*, other than the obvious things like *be*ing a child of God, *be*ing a father, and *be*ing married."

Note Garth's use of the word "do" and "be" in his answer (italicized).

Even with all the money and fame he has, he differentiated his "being" roles as his most important relationships — God and family. The "doing" happens at events while he's on the road. The "being" is in his day-in and day-out, 24/7 life. The "doing" happens in and around those roles.

Particularly in light of Scripture such as Matthew 7, we must all continually evaluate our doing versus our being. We must be honest about how we are focused on Christian *training* versus our *transformation* in Christ. Training is not proof we are transformed. But as we are being transformed, the relationship will bring about and motivate the proper training. And therefore, the actions we *do* will reflect our *being* in Him.

Always remember that God knows what you can *do*. It's the *being* He's after because that's all that will go to Heaven. Just like those elephants, we're fairly smart so the training — the doing — comes quickly; it's the relationship — the being — that takes time.

God sent him to buy freedom for us who were slaves to the law, so that he could adopt us as his very own children. And because we are his children, God has sent the Spirit of his Son into our hearts, prompting us to call out, "Abba, Father." Now you are no longer a slave but God's own child. And since you are his child, God has made you his heir. (Galatians 4:5–7)

It is not what you and I do ... It is what God is doing, and he is creating something totally new, a free life! (Galatians 6:15–*16 MSG)*

Father, I know I have a relationship with You because I am "being":

Father, one place in my spiritual life where I still tend to rely on "doing" is:

"Father, thank You for Your constant transformation of my life — Your 'being' in me. Grow me in my relationship with You to make my 'doing' out of only my love for You. Train me in Your ways in Your will to be only Your man."

Memory Verse

Now you are no longer a slave but God's own child. And since you are his child, God has made you his heir.

- Galatians 4:7 -

THE doing COMES quickly; IT'S THE RELATIONSHIP — the being — THAT TAKES time.

Congratulations on Completing 40 Days!

Everyone involved with the publishing of this book wants to encourage you to continue your new habit of spending time with God daily — reading his Word, praying, listening, journaling, applying what you hear, and growing in your faith. We want you to take the sword that is the Word of God and the shield of faith that Paul speaks of in Ephesians 6 and make a difference in the world for Christ. We pray you take in all of Jesus and live out your faith daily.

While devotional books like this are great to use, we want to challenge and encourage you to arrive at the place where you sit down every day with God's Word to read, pray, and obey. We have been given the greatest Book ever written and God has something new to say to you every day by His Spirit.

Your Heavenly Father is inviting you to join Him in His work, so stand strong, use your spiritual sword and shield, and be His ambassador in your world.

I pray that from his glorious, unlimited resources he will empower you with inner strength through his Spirit. Then Christ will make his home in your hearts as you trust in him. Your roots will grow down into God's love and keep you strong. And may you have the power to understand, as all God's people should, how wide, how long, how high, and how deep his love is. May you experience the love of Christ, though it is too great to understand fully. Then you will be made complete with all the fullness of life and power that comes from God. Now all glory to God, who is able, through his mighty power at work within us, to accomplish infinitely more than we might ask or think. Glory to him in the church and in Christ Jesus through all generations forever and ever! Amen. (Ephesians 3:16-21)

Beginning a Relationship with God Through Jesus Christ

If at any point as you went through this devotional, you had the question, “So how do I begin a relationship with God?” then first and most important, if at all possible, we recommend you talk to a pastor, priest, or mature Christian regarding this significant spiritual decision.

Here we offer you a simple explanation of the Gospel of Jesus Christ.

There is a God-shaped hole, or emptiness, inside each of us. We all try to fill this void in our own way. We cannot see on our own that God Himself is the answer to our emptiness. His Spirit has to help us.

The Bible defines sin as attitudes, thoughts, and actions that displease God. Every person since Adam and Eve has had this problem. Even if we try really hard to be “good,” we still make selfish decisions that are not pleasing to a perfect God.

In Paul’s letter to the Roman church, he created a pattern that lays out a path to salvation in Christ. For millions of people, these simple yet profound truths have led to new life.

For ever since the world was created, people have seen the earth and sky. Through everything God made, they can clearly see his invisible qualities — his eternal power and divine nature. So they have no excuse for not knowing God. Yes, they knew God, but they wouldn't worship him as God or even give him thanks. And they began to think up foolish ideas of what God was like. As a result, their minds became dark and confused. (Romans 1:20–21)

We are made right with God by placing our faith in Jesus Christ. And this is true for everyone who believes, no matter who we are. For everyone has sinned; we all fall short of God's glorious standard. Yet God, in his grace, freely makes us right in his sight. He did this through Christ Jesus when he freed us from the penalty for our sins. (Romans 3:22–24)

But God showed his great love for us by sending Christ to die for us while we were still sinners. (Romans 5:8)

For the wages of sin is death, but the free gift of God is eternal life through Christ Jesus our Lord. (Romans 6:23)

If you openly declare that Jesus is Lord and believe in your heart that God raised him from the dead, you will be saved. For it is by believing in your heart that you are made right with God, and it is by openly declaring your faith that you are saved. (Romans 10:9–10)

For "Everyone who calls on the name of the Lord will be saved." (Romans 10:13)

For everything comes from him and exists by his power and is intended for his glory. All glory to him forever! Amen. (Romans 11:36)

Countless people have begun a relationship with God through Jesus Christ after reading Paul's words guiding to salvation. This is the truth of the Gospel. But God gives you the choice. If you are ready to begin a relationship with Christ, there is a strong likelihood that there is someone in your life who would love to know, is ready to talk with you about this important choice, and answer any questions to guide you in your decision. Please talk to someone as soon as you can.

If you know that you are ready to begin a relationship with Christ right now, while there are no magic words or a specific formula for receiving God's gift of salvation, we have included a simple prayer for guidance:

"Dear God, I know I am a sinner and need Your forgiveness. I now turn from my sins and ask You into my life to be my Savior and Lord. I choose to follow You, Jesus. Please forgive my sins and give me Your gift of eternal life. Thank You for dying for me, saving me, and changing my life. In Jesus' name. Amen."

For I am not ashamed of this Good News about Christ. It is the power of God at work, saving everyone who believes — the Jew first and also the Gentile. (Romans 1:16)

Accountability Questions

Depending on the needs of your group, some of these questions you may want to answer every week, while others you may decide to switch up. Feel free to use what you like. You can also use these as a guide to write your own questions to fit your group.

Sword/Offense:

How was your relationship with God this week?

How was your Bible reading/study this week?

How was your prayer life?

Did you pray with your wife/family?

How did you grow in your marriage this week?

How did you grow as a father this week?

What is one teaching point you gained and grew from this past week?

Where was your strongest place of spiritual growth this week?

Is there a situation where you gave sacrificially?

How did you see God use you this week?

What was your greatest blessing this week?

Shield/Defense:

Was there a moment this week where you disappointed yourself?

Has any particular temptation or sin been strong in your life this week?

How have you done in your mind/thoughts this week?

Have you struggled with a sexual temptation this week? How have you fought it?

Have you committed any sexual sin?

How has your attitude been this week?

How has your mouth/speech been this week?

Did you compromise your integrity this week?

Was there a situation where you hurt or offended someone?

Was there a situation where you were a taker without regard for the other person?